Keith + ε

TESTS, TRIALS, AND TESTIMONIES

Inside Truths That Will Set You Free and Change Your Life

Trust in the Lord and keep the faith. Strive to be all God has called you to be. You are a blessing.

Patricia Hicks

Enjoy!

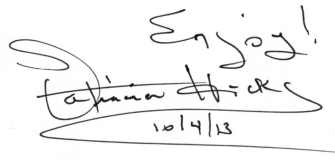

Patricia Hicks

10/4/13

PRESS

The Butterflies within this book symbolize transformation, or change, an open view that now brings beauty, love and joy, a new life, or rebirth, after having been inside a cocoon for a period of time.

TESTS, TRIALS, AND TESTIMONIES

Inside Truths That Will Set You Free and Change Your Life

Patricia Hicks

Dedication

I dedicate this book first of all to my Lord and Savior, Jesus Christ, who is the "Author" and "Finisher" of my faith. Thank You, Lord, for believing in and not giving up on me. You have been everything I need through your Holy Spirit: my Guide, my Comforter, my Teacher, my Helper, my Refuge, and my Strength. You have never left me, nor have You forsaken me. I want to proclaim to all that You are everything this world needs. I love You, Lord.

To my husband, **Mike**, who continuously loves and covers me. My love is always with you as well.

To my sons, **Mike Jr.** and **Malakesh**, and my daughters, **Melissa** and **Keela**, in life there will be tests and trials, but you will overcome them as you walk out and are doers of the Word of God. You will overcome by the blood of the Lamb and the word of your testimony. Keep your faith and trust in the Lord. Regardless of life's circumstances and challenges, you are equipped with power from on high, having the Holy Spirit in and upon you to overcome them all. As the Bible says, "Greater is he that is in you, than he that is in the world" (1 John 4:4, KJV). I call you strong in the Lord and victorious over all the works of the flesh and the devil. You are champions in Christ Jesus, His ambassador in this life. Continue in the work of the Lord, be steadfast and unmovable, and always abound in the work of the Lord. My love and prayers are always with you.

To the many people who are interested in getting insight related to tests and trials in life with the hope of having a beautiful testimony as an outcome.

Acknowledgements

Michael Hicks Sr., thank you for growing with me as we both have overcome obstacles and matured in Christ Jesus. Thank you for loving me, covering me, and for your provision. You have stood over me in the nighttime, praying over me. You have risen above life's challenges and proved yourself to be the godly man that you are called to be. Thank you for your support throughout the writing of this book. Again, thank you for loving me.

Melissa Hicks, my daughter, thank you for writing the prologue to this book and growing to be a person of perseverance.

Dorothy Latimer, thank you for having been a constant reminder to me to obey God in writing this book. You have walked this journey with me, displaying an example of trusting and having faith in God. Your life is an example of what faith looks like. You have constantly implemented a life of faith. Your friendship, prayers, listening ear, keeping in touch, and following up with me have impacted my life greatly. You are and always will be my dearest friend, one who doesn't mind being in the background, but full of faith and power. I thank God for you, and I appreciate your being in my life.

Geneva Harris, thank you for your listening ear and encouragement in the Word of God. It is evident that you are full of the Word of God. What is in a person will come out, and you let it out. I thank God that I have you to always speak truth in my life and to always point me to Jesus. I love that about you and so appreciate you for being in my life. You are a treasured friend worth keeping.

Edna Jean Allen, thank you for modeling patience and demonstrating your many love acts toward me. Thank you for being a trustworthy cousin and friend whom I will always cherish. You carry a special place in the hearts of the many people you have touched. You are a real sweetheart. I love you, Jean.

Cathy Galan, thank you for the joy that you give, songs shared, and prayers of agreement. My heart rejoice over what God is doing in and through you, my first God given Christian friend.

Yvonne Wallace, thank you for the many laughs you have given me. Laughter does good like medicine.

Principal **Mary Dwight** and teacher **Carolyn Braudrick**, thank you for taking time to proofread during your busy schedules.

Jeff Oliver, thank you for reading from a minister's perspective and giving wise and great advice. Your godliness and care are blessings to the body of Christ.

Mary Dennis and **Melissa Bogdany**, thank you for your editorial assistance, expertise, and the fresh pair of eyes, and for helping to improve the format of this book for publishing.

Betty Foster, **Madine Rogers**, **Permelia LaLonde**, and **Shirelle Baldwin**, thanks for the years of weekly faithfulness in prayer, praying unselfishly with me our foundation Scripture for all men, as illustrated in the Bible in 1 Timothy 2:1-4.

Hall-Crews, author of *GFB: "Grown Fokes Bidniss* and *Tea With Aunt Lizzie,"* you are and have been an inspiration as well as an encouragement to me.

Karen Bell, Sumrit Best, Pearl Lambert, Twanny Santokie, Lucy Seawell, Ruth Seawell, and **Curlene Williams,** thank you for joining together in faith and prayer.

Special Thanks

Shirelle Baldwin, Joyce Bethell, Bonnye Crews, Vicki Durden, Mary Dwight, Betty Foster, Geneva Harris, Judy Laws, Ivy Lindsey, Sammie Roberts, and **Caryn Ruth**, thank you for your genuine kindness and willingness to take time to review the manuscript in its entirety. You have helped sharpen another person's countenance. Your observation, insight, godly wisdom, and prayers are appreciated immensely. Thank you for believing in me and in this book. You are an inspiration and an encouragement, and I am blessed to have you in my life.

Pastor Reggie Scarborough, thank you for walking in faithfulness to your call as pastor, preaching the Word of God, that we may hear and grow spiritually by it. Thank you for being sensitive to the Spirit of the Lord's leading, keeping life in the sanctuary, and for your prayers and overseeing the people of God. We are blessed that the Lord has placed us under your leadership, and I sincerely appreciate the significance of the gift that God has given us in you. Again, thank you.

Table of Contents

Prologue

Over the years, I have watched people reach out to my mother for advice on many subjects, such as God, marriage, church, raising children, and many others. She always brought them to the Scriptures in ways to help guide them through daily struggles or even to help with their walk with God. She has always had the hand of God over her life to help guide and to impart wisdom into the lives of others.

"We do not have a High Priest who cannot sympathize with our weaknesses, but was in all points tempted as we are, yet without sin" (Hebrews 4:15). Tests and trials come to us to see how we will react to them. We are allowed tests and trial *opportunities* as proof we can stay in power over and pass the tests—not surrender by giving in to sinful manners when facing tests and trials, but have an outcome that will give us a testimony. *Tests, Trials, and Testimonies* is written for everyone to make applications in their day-to-day living.

Since I grew into a young woman, I can definitely say my mother is someone I have looked up to when seeking any type of advice. She steers me in the right direction, whether I'm right or wrong. She's a strong believer in standing up for what's right according to God's Word. Her having that thought process, I believe, is a gift from God, and it is one of the reasons why others love having her in their lives.

A few of the chapters cover God's perspective for women as wives and helpers to their husbands. Other chapters are for men and cover their taking responsibility as godly leaders. You also will read how to keep the desires of the flesh and selfishness under control. This book will help bond, strengthen, and also enlighten marriages, dating, and relationships, along with discussing how family members should have union with one another. I believe everyone—whether male, female, young, or elderly—will find something in this book that will help make a difference and change how each person may have perceived things.

—*Melissa L. Hicks*

Introduction

The purpose of this book is to help readers identify with tests and trials that take place, and I am filled with the hope that you will have a testimony as you journey to the other side of those tests and trials. The Word of God tells us, "My brethren, count it all joy when you fall into various trials, knowing that the testing of your faith produces patience" (James 1:2-3). During times of tests and trials, counting it all joy may be difficult to do. But keep the faith, knowing that "all things work together for good to those who love God, to those who are the called according to His purpose" (Romans 8:28) and that we "can do all things through Christ who strengthens" us (Philippians 4:13). In life, everyone will face tests and trials and will have to deal with them. Once you overcome them, the devil wants you to keep silent and not share that you have overcome his tactics. However, your testimonies can help set you and others free if you share them. Revelation 12:11 says, "And they overcame him by the blood of the Lamb and by the word of their testimony, and they did not love their lives to the death." Your testimony is a banner you can use to make known your victory, what the Lord has done. Your testimony demolishes the devil's work and displays his defeat. Furthermore, others are given hope and confidence to stand on the Lord's side.

The Lord dealt with me for years to write this book, and whenever I began writing, oh, how I was tested when it came to completing it. Three times, I lost my writings due to computer crashes because I did not save my material. You would think that I would have known better after the first time, or the second, and not allow it to happen *three* times. Many distractions deterred me, such as helping people accomplish things that they wanted, ministering, and doing many other good deeds. While these are good things, all these things kept me too busy to do what I was commissioned to do by the Lord. I believe in staying busy, but I was busy doing everything *but* the will of God, which was for me to write this book. It was I who needed to obey and not allow so much interference to hinder me from doing so. We all can get busy in life doing many good things, but if they are taking priority over what God has told you, something needs to be put on the back burner or cut back on. Obeying God should always be our first priority. It is better to obey God than to sacrifice. When you are ready to obey God, He will equip you with everything you need to carry out His commands. Wherever He leads you, He will provide for you! Tests and trials will come to disturb and shake you from what you are called to do. However, there is dissatisfaction within your soul and spirit when you are not in the will of God for your life. You will never feel complete until you obey Him.

As the tests and trials come, know that it is never God who tests you with evil or wrong actions. His tests will only be tests of obedience to Him. Are you ready to obey Him? Are you ready for a transformation, to see the change that you so desire? You will be given great insight in areas in which you may be tested. In this book, I also share some of my life stories as examples of the saving grace of God. With courage and your application of the Word of God to any situation in your life, you will be developed in good character, conquering all the works of the enemy, and become a testimony to others.

It was sometime in 1994 when clarity came to me to write this book. I was also given its title: *Tests, Trials, and Testimonies.* People are faced with tests and trials in everyday life. I certainly didn't want to write on the subject, for fear of rejection. I wanted to change the title of this book, but could not get away from it. Over the years, I ran to avoid this charge to write, and even justified not writing. Thoughts of being denied—fear of failure, rejection by others, shame, guilt, and more thoughts of "Who do you think you are?" and "No one cares" bombarded me. I also would think, *This book is coming from a perspective that people really don't want to hear about, which is my past experience.* Oh, the struggle within my mind held me captive to disobedience. Nevertheless, God did not change His mind. There was no escaping. I had to surrender and obey, and trust God. If He wants this book to be published, so be it. His plans for it must be to bless and inspire those who read it. Therefore, through obedience to God, prayer, and perseverance, this book you hold in your hand, *Tests, Trials, and Testimonies,* exists. All the glory goes to God!

Blessed is the one who perseveres under trial because, having stood the test, that person will receive the crown of life that the Lord has promised to those who love him. When tempted, no one should say, "God is tempting me." For God cannot be tempted by evil, nor does he tempt anyone; but each person is tempted when they are dragged away by their own evil desire and enticed. Then, after desire has conceived, it gives birth to sin; and sin, when it is full-grown, gives birth to death.

James 1:12-15 NIV

PART 1

Winning in Marriage

Married couples or anyone planning on getting married can benefit from these chapters

The First Marital Test

And now abide faith, hope, love, these three; but
the greatest of these is love.

1 Corinthians 13:13

*Author's Note: While anyone can benefit from this chapter,
it is especially helpful to married women. Whether you
have been married for a long or short time, this chapter
can help you to improve your relationship with your husband and with God.*

I have been married for more than thirty years and
believe that I have learned a few things during the
growing process of our marriage. One thing I have
learned is I love walking in peace and having peaceful
surroundings. When I married my husband, we were not
in fellowship with God; we were not living in righteousness. Although we were good people with good hearts
and were both brought up in the church, we were not
alive unto Christ at the time. Not realizing we needed
the Lord, we did our best to survive this thing called
marriage. We were young and so in love with each other,
not knowing that we needed a Savior. If your marriage
is going to survive, it will definitely take three: your
spouse, you, and, of course, God, who is first and at the
center of it all. We were always good to one another; it
was learning to live together and getting along with each

other's habits and opinions that was the challenge. Like any other couple, we eventually found out what was going to test our marriage. There were going to be some differences to deal with, and we did not always handle them in the best of ways, although we had the notion that we did. Going into the eighth month of our marriage, I rededicated my life to Jesus Christ and was very excited about the change.

For some reason, I always seemed to be under conviction during New Year's Eve, with thoughts of entering a new year and not living in right standing with the Lord. Year after year, having lived my life in a backslidden state, without fail, I would get convicted on New Year's Eve. Parents, stay encouraged. When you have trained your children in the ways they should go, they are truly ruined for sin. They are in the world, but not of it, and sooner or later, they will come to grips with this reality and come back to the ways of the Lord. In my case, just months after being married, I went to a New Year's Eve service at church and had my fellowship restored with Christ, and after midnight during the service—which was called a "watch night service"—I went home and jumped up and down on the bed like a child, telling my husband, "I am saved! I am saved! I am so happy that I am saved!"

After that night, I started to notice that my husband, Mike, was acting very differently. He became much quieter than usual and seemed to act oddly around me, and this really had me concerned. So I asked him what was going on. He said he had been thinking of what he would have to give up to be saved. I had not pressured him at all about coming to church with me, and I was so excited to hear he wanted to live for Jesus Christ along with me. God truly did a quick work in my husband; he came to church and got saved soon after my rededication to the Lord!

I figured surely we were going to make it now, for my husband was coming into a relationship with my Lord. Praise God! Mike was saved only a month after my fellowship with Christ had been restored. We were both saved and committed to living right. We were and still are Christians who love the Lord with all our hearts. I remember the first test as new Christians in our marriage. We went to a restaurant after church one night with some brothers and sisters in Christ to get something to eat and for fellowship. While the waitress was taking our orders, I tried to get her attention by calling out to her. One of the sisters said to me, "You should not holler across the table." I did not think I was loud or had "hollered." I thought I had just called out to her in a normal tone. Since we were new Christians and wanted to do what was right, my sweet, dear husband decided to side with the sister who made this comment, and corrected me in front of everyone. I quickly stood up and told him to take me home. In an authoritative tone, he said to me, "Sit down!" *Oh, no, he did not just speak to me using such a tone,* I thought. This was new, and he was not going to get away with speaking to me this way. Again, I told him to take me home, or I would walk. He just sat there, so I left the restaurant.

He came after me, thank God, to get me to come back inside. I told him I was not his child, and he would not speak to me like that, especially around other people. Again, I said to take me home now, or I was walking. He had embarrassed me, and I felt humiliated and was not going to be present in a situation like that. So, of course, we went home, and being very upset with my husband, I went to the bedroom. I prayed, asking God to help not me, but my husband to see that he had wronged me by not standing by me, but agreeing with someone else and coming against me. I thought, *I am his wife; how could he do such a thing?* I felt as if I had been attacked, and it was just not fair. I did not deserve that.

25

Sometime the next day, Mike knelt on his knees, praying to God. After a while, I heard him literally crying out to God. This was the first time I heard my husband crying, really, literally crying to God. I had never heard a man cry before. Oh, boy, did that make me feel good, because I thought he was feeling bad for what he did to me, that God was correcting him, and I had God on my side. Being a baby Christian, I thought it was good for him. *Let him cry and feel the pain in his heart that I had felt.* At that time, the Holy Spirit spoke to my heart, leading me to go to him. I responded, "Lord, You know what he did was wrong. He needs to feel what he is feeling." Yet still, my heart was impressed again to go to him, so I did, and we both in prayer together asked for forgiveness and that we would do right by each other. Little did I know that we would be tested again and also that I still had so much more to learn as a helper and as a Christian wife. I had to come to grips with the fact that my husband was God's man and my husband. The more I understood this as the years went by, the more I was able to let go of things that troubled me in our marriage and put things in proper perspective.

During this time, you could count on our being in every church service, five nights a week, sometimes six if there was a special service on Saturday. We were both always there. At times, Mike was absent due to his work schedule. We believe in being faithful to God as well as being a part of the work of the ministry in the house of the Lord, the church. Mike and I both had such a passion for being in church. Due to church being nearly every night, I desired some quality time with my husband. I made it known to him that I wanted us to spend a little time together, just him and me, outside of church activities. To my surprise, he responded, "I take you out to the church functions," and if I was not with him to step aside." What? I was baffled; this really threw me for a loop. So I told God I wanted my husband back. (Now

I've given him back to the Lord.) I was jealous of God's having my husband's attention more than I did. This sounds a little unreal, but it is the truth. I wanted some attention and some time with my husband, and I felt as though God and the church had taken my time with my husband away from me. What is so amazing about this is that later in our Christian walk, things worked in reverse, and I was the one hungering more for the things of God and church.

But my, my, my! How things have changed as time has come and gone. We are both in love with the Kingdom of God and His doings. Like me, you will have true liberty after you come to the realization that your husband truly belongs to God as well as all of us. God knows this man, His creation, so much better—therefore, trust and give him over to Him. Cast your cares over on the Lord; let go, and you will see that it will truly help you a lot when it comes to the cares, the worries related to your husband and his differences. Totally trust God for the better in your marriage. After all, He is much better at fixing things than you are. You will be set free mentally and emotionally, and you will walk in the peace of God. Hallelujah! The peace of God is so worth casting your cares over on Him. When you are carrying things, your load becomes heavier. We sometimes want our spouse to fit to our satisfaction instead of accepting that it's okay if he or she has a different stance as long as our spouse is not walking contrary to God's Word. It pays to pray and let our spouse be who he or she is. Learn to live without the gripes about little things, the complaining, and the fault-finding, all of which will not change and improve things in the way that you desire them to change. I did my best to change things for the better in our marriage, but none of my attempts produced the outcome I thought they should. It was only when I began to change, to seek the Lord, pray, and trust Him, that I began to see a transformation in our marriage. Having been tested in marriage as a Christian woman, I really thought this was going to be a relatively easy ride. What stood in the way were my flesh and the devil, and I have learned not to yield to either. Over time, growth takes place in all of us. As you surrender to the Word of God and apply it to your life, you will grow to maturity, secure in your ability to minister to the younger and other married women in the Lord. You will grow to be that example of a godly wife.

> Bid the older women similarly to be reverent and devout in their deportment as becomes those engaged in sacred service, not slanderers or slaves to drink. They are to give good counsel and be teachers of what is right and noble, so that they will wisely train the young women to be sane and sober of mind (temperate, disciplined) and to love their husbands and their children, to be self-controlled, chaste, homemakers, good-natured (kindhearted), adapting and subordinating themselves to their husbands, that the word of God may not be exposed to reproach (blasphemed or discredited).
>
> Titus 2:3-5 AMP

Focus on the Word of God, and find out what it has to say to you concerning your role as a wife, marriage, and your role of occupancy—and don't be overly concerned with changing your husband. Tests will come, whether or not you are married. And either way, you cannot change anybody, but instead, during times of trials, we should focus on personal change. What makes one think he or she can change someone else when, in fact, it's challenging to change oneself? That within itself should be a clue to allow the Holy Spirit to do what you cannot do. He can do a far better job than you can. I honor God in my marriage, and though years have passed, I still have to look to Him in all things. As the years go by, my husband and I are both continually learning and making the necessary changes for the betterment of our marriage. Seeing the Word of God more clearly helps us to line up in the path that God has designed for us, keeping us in a love that is committed regardless of the circumstances.

The Lord God is our Helper and will always be there for us as we continue this journey called marriage; till death do us part.

The test: To stay on the side of love in marriage.

The trial: The hurts and differences you have in your marriage.

The testimony: I am still standing and am now even encouraging other women in the Lord. When you are walking with God, this can be your fate as well.

Pray this prayer: *Father, thank You for having me in the place of marriage, whereby I am living with someone from whom I may learn and by whom I may grow. Keep us, I pray each day, as we continue the love walk in our marriage. I ask You for strength to do as Your Word has instructed me to do in my marriage. When times seem hard, I will look to You, for You are my Helper. I will endeavor to seek Your way of living a life of love, that others may see You through me. Thank You that I can do all things through Christ, who strengthens me. In Jesus' name I pray. Amen.*

God's Man and the Helper

And the Lord God said, "It is not good that man should be alone: I will make him a helper comparable to him."

Genesis 2:18

Have you ever wondered why God created Adam as a full-grown man instead of as a baby or a young boy first? It makes you wonder, Could this possibly be why it seems men love to be entertained and even are fascinated with what appear to be boyish things, playful games, and sports? Even their mannerisms seem to become somewhat childlike while they are involved in such events. Although every man after Adam's creation born of a woman has had those childhood experiences, there seems to be something that links them to that little boy who is no longer there in stature. Now the fully grown man side was created and has to have dominion, for it is part of his makeup, his nature. This side of him does not yearn much for others to tell him what to do. This is especially true with men's wives, who unknowingly may come across as if they are mothering them. Being told or instructed how things should be done most likely makes a man feel like a child and as if he is not in his element to rule. Okay, ladies, which do you prefer, the playful boy you may want to train all over again, or the man with leadership qualities who must take responsibility for his actions? When a wife focuses on what seems to be a lack of these qualities in her husband, although she only means to help sometimes she will verbalize her thoughts and opinions. God knew that Adam had to make a lot of decisions in life, and that he would have a great responsibility on his shoulders, more than a child could possibly handle. So Adam needed to be a man and not a child. Before God created Adam, He said:

> Let Us make man in Our image, according to Our likeness; let them have dominion over the fish of the sea, over the birds of the air, and over the cattle, over all the earth and over every creeping thing that creeps on the earth.
>
> Genesis 1:26

The Scripture says, "Let Us make *man*"—not a *child*—in the image of God. He could have made him a child and trained him Himself, but He chose not to. With that, I'd like to say, "Father knows best." Amen!

Getting back to the woman, let me role-play something familiar to you. You will have to read this in the melody of the Mighty Mouse song, when he was arriving on the scene. "Here she comes to save the day; the helpmate is on her way." Yes, the helpmate, the wife, has come to do her thing, to help, to assist, to take charge. Oops! Not so. Help as you were created to do—so the "take charge" part is out! Sometimes when helping, you may experience a few rejections, especially if the help you are offering is coming through much verbalization. You may encounter coming back at you his sharp-edged words or that body language that tells you he does not care to listen. You have to be very wise here in your reaction by practicing temperance should rejection happen. If you don't, your husband may experience your flare of emotions, which usually manifests first through the mouth, through tears, or even by way of things being thrown. You have to remain calm. You thought he was your man because he loves you, and that he would allow you to have the final say. He may or may not allow you to have the final word, but if he has indicated to you that he is not receiving what you have spoken, it really is best to get quiet. Walk away if you need to, and pray to God; after all, he is God's man. God knows how to reach him far better, for He created him and knows exactly how he ticks. God is his head and has the final say when it comes to him; therefore, let go, and let God. God can touch His heart, along with give you the wisdom you need to come across in a way in which he can receive from you. So, remain in prayer, and wait on God. Let me tell you who your husband is and his created purpose. God made him to have dominion, or authority, over the fish of the sea, the birds of the air, the cattle, all the earth, and everything that creeps on the earth. You may be thinking, *But not over me. Besides, he does not obey the Word of God, so how can you expect me to be in subjection to him? How can I consent to "the blind" leading me when he does not know where he is going or what he is doing himself?* Now, why does he think he rules over you? I encourage you to read Genesis 3:1-24. For now, I'm going to highlight the part that God said to Eve after she and Adam disobeyed God's commandment by eating the forbidden fruit.

To the woman He said: "I will greatly multiply your sorrow and your conception; in pain you shall bring forth children; your desire shall be for your husband, and he shall rule over you."

Genesis 3:16

Here is when the husband was given the authority, the say, a statement of what to do and what not to do, an order over his wife. This does not imply that you are to be treated like a doormat, physically or verbally abused, or walked all over. That is not what God is saying here. Perhaps your husband is not sensitive to your needs or has some areas that may need improvement. In order for you to see the change you want to see in your husband, someone has to be the first to change, and characteristically, it is the woman being in submission to win him over. Why is it the woman? Simply put, she has the capability to help him as long as she has made an adjustment to her role. He will change in time because if change happens in her, change will occur within him; he has to meet her in the change.

Sometimes wives tend to love so much, along with possibly thinking, *If they would only listen, hear, and understand what we are saying, it could deliver them from not only their troubles, but also ours, or even the entire household's troubles.* Women are nurturers who help take care of things. We have the ability to care for, to rear, bring up, and train in addition to educating others on how just about everything should be done. In other words, we do have our outlook on things in addition to being glad to help by giving our advice. You may be an exception, but typically, most women are that way by nature. After all, God made a wife to be a helpmate, to be there to help, specially made for the husband, and should that help be refused, the wife may feel rejected. If only husbands would realize what they truly have—a good thing to help make things better. Hmm! Allow me to think here for a moment. I sure would like some help around here. Who would deny some help? Hmm . . . could it be a man? Is it men's pride or macho character? Let me clarify; I'm not saying that help from a wife is always refused or rejected. I'm just speaking in general about the nature of a man to lead compared with the nature of a woman to help, and how it sometimes gets misconstrued as to who is having the final say. Father

God gave a helper to the husband, and wouldn't you say, "Father knows best"? I have learned to thank God that my husband is God's man. He created my husband, so let God deal with him, is my conclusion. It means less work for me. Let God be God to your husband, and you work on becoming a better you and a better helper.

With patience and change occurring within you, most definitely change will happen within your marriage. To see change take place in your relationship, *you* must first change by fulfilling your responsibility according to the Scriptures given to wives. In return, you will have your husband facing a changed, new you. Observing and living with this change ultimately will cause change to occur in him. How? Change is good to build upon, and it's a course of action to which people are used to responding. Therefore, when your husband sees and likes the new you, the hidden person of the heart, with the incorruptible beauty of a gentle and quiet spirit, he will desire it and draw near to that newness. As long as the alteration is God's way of doing things, it will give you great dividends. But there has to be an *internal* change that takes place before you will see an *external* change take place. Renew your mind with the Word of God; renew within. That change needs to work from the inside out, not the outside in. We can make change within ourselves; however, we cannot change others, for change is something they have to want for themselves.

Changing from your way of doing things does not always feel pleasant to your flesh, but when the pain of remaining the same outweighs the pain of change, will you change? Do you really want change? Are you willing to pay the price for it? Change is just an adjustment to a way of doing things, yet it seems to be somewhat difficult at times. Why is that? The answer is simple: It's selfishness. Most people want things their way because the flesh desires to have its way. It's amazing when someone does not see things from our point of view how quickly we can believe that they are the ones who need to make the adjustments and change. However, you must accept the fact that you and your spouse are two totally different people called to different assignments in the marriage. Now, I do believe women should express to their husbands and share with their husbands freely concerning any situation, at least once, but know when to leave it alone. Depending on your husband's response, you may have to drop the subject at hand and allow the greater One—God—to deal with his heart. Good things to do if rejection should happen are study to be quiet, pray, and, most of all, learn how to speak to your husband without criticism. It will be far more effective to admire him, build him up, and use gentleness along with calmness in your speech than to tear him down with emotional words and contentiousness.

> A soft answer turns away wrath, but a harsh word stirs up anger. The tongue of the wise uses knowledge rightly, but the mouth of fools pours forth foolishness. . . . A wholesome tongue is a tree of life, but perverseness in it breaks the spirit.
>
> Proverbs 15:1-2, 4

Men, along with others, can be on the defensive whenever the word "you" is used. For example, "You always . . ." or "You never . . . ." When in discussions, how you use the word "you" has the possibility of backfiring on YOU! No one likes fingers in his or her face, not even you. (You can read more on this subject in part 2, "Overcome and Live Victoriously," in the chapter "Facing the Finger.") If expressions are coming through negative emotions, along with fault-finding words, the results can be negative. "Do not be deceived, God is not mocked; for whatever a man sows, that he will also reap" (Galatians 6:7). Giving positive words reaps a positive reaction. Which do you prefer? What you put out is what you will get in return.

Men are hunters. They chase, and as a result, it is good for them to have a little curiosity about your behavior that causes them to think. So if you are used to responding negatively or by finding fault, try a different approach; do it God's way. God created man and gave him dominion, the say, the authority. You may have already observed that it is in him to reign in his authority. Even if he does it in a quiet way, he is going to be in charge in his own way. It's in his nature as well as that of anyone who is set in an authoritative position. We see this authority in all regions of life where there is one in a position of authority. It may be in the church, a business or workplace, the military, or the government. It is known that in leadership positions, the people under the authority figures are not the ones giving the guidelines for how things will be done, but vice versa. There is in all walks of life someone who is set in authority. We are, at most, expected to be in obedience to what is set before us, but we do have a free will, a choice of whether or not to follow the leading, ordinance, or regulation. Being in the comfort of your home does not permit the chain of command to be any different; who's in authority remains the same. We are to do likewise, as servants are in submission to their masters.

[You who are] household servants, be submissive to your masters with all [proper] respect, not only to those who are kind and considerate and reasonable, but also to those who are surly [overbearing, unjust, and crooked]. For one is regarded favorably [is approved, acceptable, and thankworthy] if, as in the sight of God, he endures the pain of unjust suffering. [After all] what kind of glory [is there in it] if, when you do wrong and are punished for it, you take it patiently? But if you bear patiently with suffering [which results] when you do right and that is undeserved, it is acceptable and pleasing to God. For even to this were you called [it is inseparable from your vocation]. For Christ also suffered for you, leaving you [His personal] example, so that you should follow in His footsteps. He was guilty of no sin, neither was deceit [guile] ever found on His lips.

1 Peter 2:18-22 AMP

I know this may sound pretty insensitive, possibly will be hard on the flesh, and may not feel fair, but it is written in the Bible, illustrating an example of submission to those who are in authority.

There is hope, so rejoice and be glad. In the next chapter I will show you the victory side of such submission.

The test: Having a husband as the one in authority and you as the helper.

The trial: Accepting his role, his worth, and his position by giving him reverence with submission.

The testimony: I have accepted the divine order: God, a husband in authority, and the helper. As the helper, I have entered into peace, knowing that it is not my responsibility to change my husband or anyone. I have changed to be better in my relationship with God and my love walk. Casting all my cares on the Lord, for He cares for me, has given me a new outlook on life.

Pray this prayer: *Thank You, Father, for loving me and giving me a husband who is leading. I pray and ask You for continual understanding, wisdom, and acceptance of who my husband is in Christ Jesus. Father, with the help* *of the Holy Spirit, I will do my part as the helpmate that You have called me to be. Father, my trust is in You to work things out for the good of both my husband and me in our marriage. I will reverence my husband with all due respect and will function in the part delegated to me. Father, that I may show honor to You in obedience to Your Word, I will speak softly and use kind words during conversations with my husband. Help me, Father, to be sensitive and know when to hold back my words and just give myself in prayer. Help me to let go and let You have Your way, Father. In Your precious Son Jesus' name I pray. Amen.*

God's Man or My Man?

> . . . rather let it be the hidden person of the heart, with the incorruptible beauty of a gentle and quiet spirit, which is very precious in the sight of God.
>
> 1 Peter 3:4

Thank God for the Holy Spirit and the Word of God helping us to carry out our delegated role as a help-mate. In this chapter, I am speaking specifically to the wife (not to the husband) who may not have been acting in her God-given role as a helpmate and desires to do so. With wives, I sometimes think our role is to help soften the heart of our husband in some areas, to help give balance, along with a reflection of the love of God. I often have said this concerning the husbands: "They are the head, but we are the neck to turn it," which is an analogy of the ability within you to truly help turn him toward God. Choose to put yourself in the right position according to the Word of God by doing as it is written, and see that it really is God who turns his attention toward Himself.

> Wives, likewise, be submissive to your own husbands, that even if some do not obey the word, they, without a word, may be won by the conduct of their wives, when they observe your chaste conduct accompanied by fear. Do not let your

adornment be merely outward—arranging the hair, wearing gold, or putting on fine apparel— rather let it be the hidden person of the heart, with the incorruptible beauty of a gentle and quiet spirit, which is very precious in the sight of God. For in this manner, in former times, the holy women who trusted in God also adorned themselves, being submissive to their own husbands, as Sarah obeyed Abraham, calling him lord, whose daughters you are if you do good and are not afraid with any terror.

1 Peter 3:1-6

From the above Scripture passage, I will be expounding and emphasizing these words: **submissive, do not obey, without a word, won,** and **conduct.** You see, **submissive** is a strong word having to do with releasing control to another, yielding to someone else's power, and giving authority to another. A wife may think her husband may not be doing his God-given part and so is not worthy of her submission. You may be thinking, *How can I allow that when he does **not obey** the Word of God? You mean allow him to lead when he may not be spiritually leading according to the Scriptures? You are joking, right?* No, I am not joking, just giving you biblical facts. I must say you are not to follow him or anyone in sin and wrongdoing contrary to the Word of God. Do what's right, and believe God will work things out for both of you. You are a believer, right? Believers believe, and he who believes enters into rest, according to Scripture.

For we which have believed do enter into rest, as he said, As I have sworn in my wrath, if they shall enter into my rest: although the works were finished from the foundation of the world.

Hebrews 4:3 KJV

Rest assured, the Word of God works, if you choose to work the Word. Remember that your husband is God's man; he belongs to God, and He knows him best, and knows it is good that man is not alone. As a result, it is not a mistake that you are his helpmate. Let me say also that I do not believe, nor am I indicating, that a wife in an abusive state should submit to that standard of living.

I sense that this moment is one to stop and say if you are reading this book and have not accepted Jesus Christ as Lord and Savior of your life, stop right now and ask Jesus to come into your heart by saying this aloud: "I believe that Jesus Christ is the Son of God. I believe that He died on the cross for me and He arose from the grave on the third day. I believe this with my heart and confess it with my mouth and call Jesus Christ my Lord and Savior. Father God, come live in my heart and save me from sin and my way of doing things. I believe and receive forgiveness of my sins and receive Jesus Christ as my Lord and my Savior." Praise God! Hallelujah! Welcome to the family of God.

It really takes God's being in your life to give you the strength, along with His wisdom, to do what must be done to be God's woman for God's man. You belong to God, and He has sent His Holy Spirit to help you and also to comfort you in times of need. Find a good, strong local church that teaches the truth of God's Word to help you in your everyday walk with Jesus Christ. If you really and truly want to be the helper God has ordained you to be in your marriage, you must become a doer, not just a hearer, of the Word of God. It is in the *doing* that the job gets done. You have the power and capability within you to win your husband over without manipulation.

First must come **submission**. Surrender the power to him. I am not saying to be his doormat, allowing him to walk all over you and mistreat you. Nor am I indicating that you should be in an abusive situation;

I do not believe that is what the word **submission** is saying. However, allow him to be the man, for that is what he is, the man set in authority. To broaden your understanding of the word **submission**, look at these synonyms: obedience, compliance, surrender, acquiescence, consent, a giving in, deference, assent, and agreement. Ouch! You may feel uncomfortable about the word **submission**, but it really is meant for good and is not as bad as your flesh may feel. To do anything that is contrary is to show resistance, opposition, a battle, a struggle or fighting against, and even rebellion, and all are what you don't want to yield to. Letting go may not always feel pleasurable to your flesh, but it will turn out all right for you both. Looking to God to go to the heart of His man to make the necessary changes, you will win if you work the Word. Women who are inclined to know what to do, along with how things should be done, usually do not have a problem expressing themselves to their husbands. I sometimes wonder if that is why the words that God had to say to Eve were, "Your desire will be for your husband, and he shall rule (have authority) over you." Her right to rule, or to have the final say, was out. She ate the fruit and then gave it to her husband to eat, and this was in direct disobedience to what God had commanded. When you look at the Scripture concerning this, you will see that God spoke to the man specifically, not to the woman, regarding what tree he could and could not eat of:

> Then the Lord God took the man and put him in the Garden of Eden to tend and keep it. And the Lord God commanded the man, saying, "Of every tree of the garden you may freely eat; but of the tree of the knowledge of good and evil you shall not eat, for in the day that you eat of it you shall surely die."
>
> Genesis 2:15-17

According to the written Scriptures, Eve was not yet created during the time that God gave Adam these instructions, although clearly you can see that after her creation, she had to have been informed by God or Adam. Her conversation with the serpent can be observed as proof that she was knowledgeable about the forbidden fruit.

Now the serpent was more cunning than any beast of the field which the Lord God had made. And he said to the woman, "Has God indeed said, 'You shall not eat of every tree of the garden'?" And the woman said to the serpent, "We may eat the fruit of the trees of the garden; but of the fruit of the tree which is in the midst of the garden, God has said, 'You shall not eat it, nor shall you touch it, lest you die.'"

Genesis 3:1-3

She knew the instructions God had given, for she told the serpent what could and could not be eaten. So she knew, right? On the other hand, Adam did not speak up and take a stand to obey God's instructions. He allowed his wife to override him and moreover influence him to disobey what God had said. God, being omniscient— meaning "knowing everything; also with complete and infinite knowledge"—knew that this ability of the woman to influence man into disobedience also could influence man to walk in obedience to Him. How? In opposition of what she did **"without a word."**

Eve went as far as overriding God's authority and ate the fruit. She also gave to her husband "with her", and he ate (Genesis 1:6), as if what God had said were not true. If Adam, being "with her", had spoken up during the serpent's conversation with his wife, the disobedience could have been stopped. The consequences set in place the arrangement predestined by God for the marriage. Many women have probably thought, *Ouch, Eve! Why did you do that?* If she could, she probably would ask you the same question: Why do you do that? Is it the nature of the woman? However, now that you are put in the place of **submission**, a price, to some extent, has to be paid. Deny yourself from speaking much, yet within this same occurrence win God's man over if he does *not obey* the Word of God. Remember, Adam did **not obey**, nor did he take a stand on God's Word, but he ate the fruit given to him by the woman, knowing it was forbidden. At times, it may seem that your husband is not hearing much of what you are saying anyway. The word **submission** can be powerful and can have a greater and more effective influence.

Obtain success in marriage by your husband's watching your **conduct**, your behavior activated God's way. Don't speak quickly in correction, but speak slowly in wisdom. It really is as uncomplicated as the Bible says if you are willing to pay the price of keeping quiet. "What?" You may say. "Why can't I tell him what I feel?" There are times for that, but sometimes it's best to be quiet or slow to speak. Pray and seek God's wisdom for the matter. If your husband does *not obey* the Word of God, the Word says he will be **"won."** How? First, **"without a word"** implies that you are not talking. You can control your speech and hold all those words back. Oh, yes, you can. You would not have been given this instruction if you were not capable of doing so.

Here is an illustration of your getting control of yourself. Someone you respect highly as your pastor, a minister, a parent, a grandparent, or a teacher, or anyone you look up to suddenly walks up during an out-of-control "mouth episode." You stop instantly, in the midst of expressing your feelings to your husband, or badgering or nagging him. More than likely, you will stop immediately and, **without a word** spoken to him, get a grip on yourself, controlling your behavior. Why do you give more respect to others, not wanting them to hear and see this behavior, than you do to God, who sees all the time? God has given the solution, which is the reverse of much talking. It sounds like your actions speak louder than your words. Watch your behavior, for it is very important for the task of winning him over. Let's read the first two verses again from the Amplified Bible.

> In like manner, you married women, be submissive to your own husbands [subordinate yourselves as being secondary to and dependent on them, and adapt yourselves to them], so that even if any do not obey the Word [of God], they may be won over not by discussion but by the [godly] lives of their wives, when they observe the pure and modest way in which you conduct yourselves, together with your reverence [for your husband; you are to feel for him all that reverence includes: to respect, defer to, revere him—to honor, esteem, appreciate, prize, and, in the human sense, to adore him, that is, to admire, praise, be devoted to, deeply love, and enjoy your husband].
>
> 1 Peter 3:1-2 AMP

This is plain, simple and to the point, so anyone can understand what is being said here. Tell yourself you can do this, and just do it again, and again, and again. You will win if you do not get weary and give up. Your faith in action will give you the outcome you really want to have. We are getting from the Word of God what it takes to win God's man over into obedience. You can do it! The world, the flesh, and the devil will tell you to have it your way or hit the highway, or if it gets too hard, to get out of it, get a divorce, and get another husband. It's effortless to move by your flesh or emotions, but putting your flesh under subjection to the

Holy Spirit takes an effort to yield. Try it God's way; it's so much better, and you will see that victory is on your side. Loving and respecting your husband does not exclude trials. Marriage is not always a bed of roses; it takes WORK to work the Word. Many times, you will have to get yourself out of the way, along with keeping a peace of mind. Enter the rest of God knowing that eventually you will win. Stay in obedience to the Word of God in faith, knowing that the "now faith is the substance of things hoped for, the evidence of things not seen" (Hebrews 11:1).

There was a time in my life when, with right intentions, I tried to change my husband. I did the talking, really expressing myself to him with sincerity, with love and affection, as well as with emotions. I told my husband that I would never do anything to hurt him or our marriage, and honestly I never will. I was only trying to help and did not understand why he refused my help . . . and I told him this. His reply was that I was trying to break him. *Huh? What is wrong with this man? Has he lost his mind? I am his wife, his helpmate. What? Trying to break him!* The honest, heartfelt rationale in my mind was only to offer him help. Oh, no! In his mind, I was trying to break his will. *Again, what is wrong with this man? Why doesn't he see and understand that I am trying to help for the better? I am through with this. We are so different, and maybe we are not meant to be together.* All of these thoughts rushed through my brain. You see, there were different perceptions here. He is a man, God's man, and his way of thinking was different from mine. Oh, yes, I really did see that he needed to change if this marriage was going to work. God said for him to love me, and if he did, he needed to do some changing. Like a bull, of course, he was not budging—for he was the man in charge. When opportunity presented itself—not every now and then, but every now and again, and again, and again—I tried to help him through much verbalization. I was no quitter, and I didn't give up hope for change. I didn't take a pushy or overbearing approach. No, more than kindheartedly and with soft speaking, I was determined that this man of God would see and receive my help. Yet once more, he implied that I was trying to break and change him. Finally, I got fed up with talking and just got quiet. After I was quiet for a while, he asked me what was wrong, and then alleged that I was trying to make him feel guilty by being quiet. Then I felt no matter what I did or said, I was the one in the wrong. In the car coming from church one day and feeling spiritual with the belief that he would receive from me at that point, I began talking with him about what I thought was a helpful subject. But after feeling as if I was not getting anywhere in the conversation, I stopped talking. He was not used to my silence, so he abruptly implied that I was trying to make him feel guilty. This time, being agitated, I, surprisingly out of character, said to him with a sturdy voice, "I DON'T CARE WHAT YOU THINK," and from that day, I surrendered myself to change. I was through. God probably applauded and thought, *"It's about time."*

I caught myself not having much to say (**without a word**) about things or my feelings anymore. I found comfort in making adjustments in my thinking, renewing my mind with the Word of God. Without being angry or having any ill feelings toward my husband, I found myself entering peace within my heart, soul, and mind. Never having had an argumentative type of personality, it was quite easy for me to go about in peace. I'd rather pay the price in denying myself the possibility of winning through words and instead walk in and have the peace of God anytime. It is far better to choose peace and tranquility over a tormented mind from wanting to be right. Do you want to be right, or do you want to win? Why not both? Be right (if you feel you are) quietly, **without a word** spoken, and also win doing it God's way. In the physical realm, you do not have to fight to be right—you only have to "fight the good fight of faith" mentioned in 1 Timothy 6:12. Remember to put your armor on (Ephesians 6:11), and never take it off.

> For we do not wrestle against flesh and blood, but against principalities, against powers, against the rulers of the darkness of this age, against spiritual hosts of wickedness in the heavenly places.
>
> Ephesians 6:12

Now, this change of behavior that had taken place was being observed by my husband, who was not at all used to it. He would say to me that I was trying to make him feel bad because now I was quiet and not the talkative person he knew. I held steady and did not let this disturb my peace. I knew that going there with him would be a setup to entangle me again through words. No matter what he said to challenge me, I did not go there. I had been there, done that. Instead, I stayed on course and refused to allow the enemy to get to my emotions, or get me upset and releasing my feelings. I was focused and determined to change *me*, not him. To help me, I studied all the Scriptures in the Bible intended for a wife to be sure of my responsibilities and how I was to **conduct** myself. Since I hadn't seen change over the years of offering help through my words, I resolved to surrender to the Word of God to have soundness in our marriage. I realized through the knowledge of the Word of God that the answer was always there, waiting to be applied in my life. Indeed, the prescription **"without a word"** is the correct way to behave, not all the talking, wearing yourself out.

It was a bit hard on my flesh at times, but I set my flesh aside and submitted to obedience to the Word of God. Becoming a doer of the Word of God, with help from the Holy Spirit, I found out that I do not always have to speak what I am thinking or feeling. **Conduct** (in righteousness) says to me that your actions speak louder than your words; it is, beyond a doubt, liberating. As a matter of fact, over a period of time, my **conduct** spoke volumes to my husband—it spoke much more effectively than my words ever had done. The manifestation that he witnessed was a real change in the way I **conducted** myself. He had observed the change in me, and he now had to live with that change. He also had to face, react, respond, and move toward the change he saw. This change ultimately caused him to change his approach and also draw near to God. Along with this, he had more consideration toward me. Hallelujah! It seems as if the change, the difference in the internal beauty that had taken place, was speaking much louder than what formerly showed up externally, and that change caused my husband to be attracted to the inner beauty.

So, you see, **without a word** and working the Word, I ultimately **won.** Do know that I did have communication with my husband. I am not saying that you cannot talk and have discussions with your husband. You should be able to talk freely with your husband in everyday life; just take notice when he is receiving from you and when he is having the final say. This may sound like the Word is asking a lot from you and may be hard on your flesh, but trust and obey, and do it God's way (a great dividend). Anything that pays will cost you something. If you have been faithfully doing all according to this Scripture text for quite some time and have not seen any results, stay faithful; it surely will come to pass. Examine yourself, and make sure your husband consistently sees the change. The Scripture says he will be **won.** You may ask, "When?" Let's read again verse 2 from the Amplified version, which specifies when what husbands observe indicates they must see something.

When they observe the pure and modest way in which you conduct yourselves, together with your reverence [for your husband; you are to feel for him all that reverence includes: . . . to honor, esteem, appreciate, prize, and, in the human sense, to adore him, that is, to admire, praise, be devoted to, deeply love, and enjoy your husband].

1 Peter 3:2 AMP

This verse really spells it out for us and says it all. Ask yourself if your husband is observing. Does he really see these traits in you? Is your conduct pure and modest? Are you giving reverence to him? Are you honoring, esteeming, appreciating, prizing, and adoring him? Are you praising him? Are you devoted to him? Do you deeply love and enjoy your husband? He needs to see this in your behavior before he can be **won.** God's man *is* given with instructions. Putting the Word into action will cause you to be victorious. Decide today that you will do it God's way. If you have not been a doer of the Word of God in the past, do your part, and don't concern yourself so much with your husband's doing his part. If you desire to see changes, then accept first that change must begin within someone. Are you someone? Your marriage really and truly can survive through the influence and help of the wife in **submission.**

I used to catch my husband watching me with curiosity, not knowing what to expect. I kept reading the Bible, played Christian music in our home, watched Christian television, prayed a lot, and raised our children. All that gave me another focus, and it can for you also. Let your husband see you do some of the same things: listening to Christian music and watching Christian television, for example. Let him see you praying on your knees. His observation of these things will speak and point his attention also toward God. Remember you are **without a word** to him. You are especially not criticizing him if he is not doing these things. His heart, not your mouth, eventually will convict him.

Need to talk? Ask God to put some Christian friends in your life. When I really, really wanted to talk, the Lord placed two good, solid Christian lady friends in my life, in whom I could confide, and who listened to, encouraged, and ministered to me. You should always want someone who will tell you the truth and not just what you want to hear.

Sing, and make a melody in your heart to the Lord. Get in a place of intimacy with the Lord. He is your Abba Father (Daddy God). No one will love you like He does. Lean on and trust in Him, for He is your Refuge, your Source of help, and your Comfort. Living and having a peaceful life in harmony with each other is a great goal for your marriage. During adversity, learn how to look at your husband and smile while staying in peace. Do not be moved by what you feel or your circumstances. Totally surrender all concerning your husband and your marriage without a silent treatment that is cold or with malice of heart.

Once you totally submit, it's a cinch to keep peace, harmony, and change. My husband and I really got along just fine, for the most part; we really are a fun couple. When he comments about how he feels about certain things, I simply nod my head, agree, and even openly discuss with him his view or help him with his vision, his insight. Sometimes I will throw in my opinion, and if he responds abruptly or differently from what I expected, I get quiet. Instead of responding emotionally, trying to persuade him to see it my way, I just get quiet and/or sometimes just walk away, putting my attention on something else without getting upset with him. I have learned how to redirect my brain from one thought to another, renew my mind with the Word of God. Finally, I got it! He is God's man and not mine to handle, so casting cares over to the Lord to deal with him was gratifying. In my lifetime, arguing has never been my forte. I do not like to even be in an argumentative environment, much less participate in it. I prefer peace anytime, and if it takes leaving an issue alone to have peace, then peace I can do. Nevertheless, my husband was never mean to me. He was then, and still is, a very good man. I have just come into the revelation that he is indeed a man, and he is, and always will be, God's man; to God he has to answer.

It took between seven and ten years of marriage for me to learn to shut up, zip my lip, know when to speak and when not to, and to pray like it depends on God. So should you feel rejection, or even feel like the odd couple at times, just do your part; do what is right. Study and search out all the Scriptures with the words "wife," "mother," and "woman," and become a doer of the Word, for in time, change will happen. The sooner you obey, the closer you are to winning.

Let me give you a paradigm to remember should you ever feel like you're in danger of launching into what could be a long outburst. A parent has told her young children to put away their toys. They continue to play, showing disobedience. At the same time, they are telling the parent something like, "No! Not yet. Okay, in a little while" or "We are not quite finished yet." Maybe a teenager was told that he or she can go to a special event, but is not allowed to drive the car and is given a curfew. The now-frustrated teenager does not like this and immediately responds, justifying why the teenager should have it his or her way. Responses include: "You don't trust me. Why do I have to come home so early? Johnny's parents let him drive their car. I will be careful. Why are you treating me this way?" Becoming very upset, the teenager leaves the house, slamming the door. The teenager does not show up at the given curfew, but an hour later.

Let's use the same bold characterization concerning the wife to appropriately point out a principle using both the young children and the teenager. There was no **submission** to authority, the parent's instruction. They refused to receive the parent's spoken word and act in obedience. Instead, they had rebellious **conduct**; the children **did not obey** their parent. They talked back, and were not **without a word** to the one in authority. The teenager even slams the door before he or she leaves the house. Maybe with a manner consistent with the wife in **submission** and obedience, they, too, may have **won** some favor here with the parent. Perhaps the feeling the parent got is exactly what the husband feels when his wife is in a continual talking mode. Talking back is what we call it when children are retaliating against instructions. Yes! It's called talking back. Are you talking back to your husband?

It amazes me how some parents tolerate this. I, myself, have been guilty of this tolerance. So why do we feel our husbands should put up with this? Like the sound of a constantly dripping faucet, it can really be annoying. Look at the New King James Version of the Bible to see what the Word of God is saying about this behavior in a woman.

Better to dwell in a corner of a housetop, than in a house shared with a contentious woman.
Proverbs 21:9; Proverbs 25:24

Obviously, it is not good to be around this behavior because in this Scripture, it clearly says it is better to be "in a corner of a housetop"! Wow! Isn't that on the roof? Interestingly, it's stated to be in the corner of it. That says a lot about the keyword *contentious*, which means "fond of arguing and given to disputing and quarrelsome." Purpose in your heart that you will be a doer of the Word and exercise the biblical principles to win your husband, as stated earlier in 1 Peter 3:1-3. As a wife and a woman, have you ever asked, "Why is this directed to the women? What about the men who may have this contentious problem?" After much reading of the Scriptures related to the wife's role along with living with God's man (my husband), I have become convinced that the wife is truly the helpmate. Just think, God gave the wife the ability to win him over, but it will only happen when you do your part and, of course, pray. Over the years, I have stated that a lot (referring here to a bunch) falls on the woman's lot (referring here to her ground or portion). To further enlighten you as to who you are, let's read from a text from the Amplified version.

Every wise woman builds her house, but the foolish one tears it down with her own hands. He who walks in uprightness reverently and worshipfully fears the Lord, but he who is contrary and devious in his ways despises Him. In the fool's own mouth is a rod [to shame] his pride, but the wise men's lips preserve them.

Proverbs 14:1-3

Picture this. An architect sits inside a comfort-controlled building designing blueprints, but the builder gets out in the heat for the construction, working hard to create a manifestation of what is on the blueprint. A wise woman can eliminate the hard work by building on solid ground; that solid ground is the Word of God. To build on anything less will cause a great deal of heartache, especially when contentiousness tears down what was meant to be built up. Words can be used to build someone up or tear the person down.

He who guards his mouth preserves his life, but
he who opens wide his lips shall have destruction.

Proverbs 13:3

Death and life are in the power of the tongue, and
those who love it will eat its fruit.

Proverbs 18:21

Watch what comes out of your mouth; it produces
death or life . . . so choose cautiously. Understand that
most husbands have little understanding, knowledge,
or even the skills to meet their wives' needs. It is okay
to tell him what it is you need from him. If he does
not provide it, then continually pray, and stand on the
Word of God. Stay positive, and assure him that you
believe in him. Ask him for his advice or opinions sometimes—it makes him feel respected and valued. He may
need to know that you respect his decisions. You do not
always have to agree with him; just do not be so quick
to disagree, especially when his decision is not going to
hurt anyone. Why knock it? Praise him for his efforts
and for the work he does that helps provide for the
household. He will gravitate toward your admiration of
him, so appreciate, respect, and revere him. Sometimes
just forget about your feelings and build him up. Call
those things that are not, into existence in the areas
where you would like to see him grow stronger. Show
him sometimes that you are interested in what interests
him. The playful, boyish side of him is a good start. In
time, you will reap rewards. He loves you; after all, he
married you. So be the helpmate by coming alongside
him and helping him be the man of God that he was
created to be.

Keep in mind whose man he really is, God's or yours.
He is God's man, and accepting that releases you from
the frustration of trying to make him all over. God has
created him as His man to have dominion over all the

earth and, in addition, authority over the woman. No matter how hard you may try, it cannot be changed, reversed, redone, or recreated. God said it; the arrangement is set, and if you fight it, you will lose.

You may have heard women use the words "my man" or "your man." *My* and *your,* imply that we possess something. The words "my husband" and "your husband" only state their titles, which you can possess or take hold of. When you say "my man," it identifies him as a person, a human being, and truth be told, we do not possess, or own, human beings. So whose man is he? He is indeed God's man, for He created him. God has the power and the authority over him. He belongs to God, and with humility and obedience to the Word of God, you can be made whole and free of any worries in your marriage by being the helpmate that you are ordained to be. Be the beacon of light, and when he observes your demeanor, it will direct him to Him who is every man's head, the man Christ Jesus.

As an older woman with years of studying the Scriptures pertaining to marriage, I trust that this chapter has been good counsel in "what is right and noble," and trust you will choose to be "sane and sober of mind (temperate, disciplined)" and that you will love your husbands and your children, that you will be "self-controlled, chaste, homemakers, good-natured (kindhearted), adapting and subordinating" yourselves to your own husbands, "that the word of God may not be exposed to reproach (blasphemed or discredited)" (Titus 2:3-5 AMP).

The test: Submission and obedience to the Word of God.

The trial: Controlling the mouth without words.

The testimony: Having won your husband over into the obedience of God, and with the acceptance that it's okay to be different, winning God's way and living carefree.

Pray this prayer: *Father, I ask You to help me become all that You will have me to be. Help me to be pleasing in Your sight by being a doer, not just a hearer, of the Word. I ask You to give me wisdom to do what needs to be done according to Your Word as a wife to my husband, (his name), so that my husband, (his name), will observe the hidden person of my heart, the incorruptible beauty of a gentle and quiet spirit, which is very precious in Your sight, God. Father, I will trust You to do Your part as I activate my faith not looking at what I see or hear in the natural, but what I read, see, and hear in the spirit of Your Word. I thank You, Father, that what You have joined together in my husband, (his name), and me no man, including us, will put asunder. I surrender all to You, and I will trust You with all my heart and not lean to my own understanding. I pray and ask You for strength to do Your will, and I thank You that my husband loves me like Christ loves the church and he gives himself to me. I thank You and believe that I have received all that I have asked You. In your Son Jesus' name I pray. Amen!*

Man of God, Where Are You?

Then the Lord God called to Adam and said to him, "Where are you?"

Genesis 3:9

W hy did God have to ask Adam, "Where are you?" Was it to see if Adam would recognize that he had hidden himself from his responsibility and did not want to face his obligation to carry out what was given him? One thing is for sure, God knew exactly where Adam was. The question is, Did Adam recognize where he was? Adam knew he was in a condition of disobedience, and therefore, he hid himself. Most people who have done something wrong do not want to be caught, so they attempt to hide from the individual in authority, the law, or whoever has established the order they are supposed to obey. When the authoritative figure is not present, sometimes there is mischief, a behavior that can cause harm or trouble. Let's look at some incidents of the adage "When the cat's away, the mouse will play" from the perspective of having a boss, teacher, or parent who has been temporarily out of sight from those who report to him or her.

When the person in authority comes back to the scene, there is usually a sudden move to either hide or to get back in position to conform to expected behavior. People are not the only ones who hide; even animals have an instinct to hide. A dog owner can verify that when his or her pet has gotten into some sort of mischief. The pet will hide when the master shows up. The pet may even have a sorrowful look on its face. Not wanting to be caught or to face the wrong they have done, both people and animals may show embarrassment, guilt, or fear. There is something in our nature that does not want us to be exposed for wrongdoing.

Here are just a few examples of people who commit sins or are guilty of wrongdoing and do not want to be caught: cheating spouses, criminals who do not want to do the time, students cheating on homework or tests, children involved in horseplay in a classroom, and employees doing something other than what is listed in their work descriptions. People walking in the flesh naturally want the pleasure of sin without dealing with its consequences. Adam and Eve's knowledge that they were naked caused them to be afraid. Could it possibly also be that they hid themselves because they did not want to be accountable for their actions? Notice that when God called out, it was Adam He called and not Eve. When God put Adam into the Garden of Eden, He gave him instructions to obey, for Eve had not yet been created. So Adam, the man of God, was the one who received the instructions, and he was responsible for following them.

> Then the Lord God took the man and put him in the garden of Eden to tend and keep it. And the Lord God commanded the man, saying, "Of every tree of the garden you may freely eat; but of the tree of the knowledge of good and evil you shall not eat, for in the day that you eat of it you shall surely die."
>
> Genesis 2:15-17

These verses indicate God is speaking directly to Adam. As you read further, you will see that it was after God had spoken these words that Eve was created, which unmistakably lets us know that Eve was not present, and therefore, Adam had the responsibility of making sure that what God had spoken would be carried out obediently. God's created man was given instructions up to where he was in life at that moment. Adam's only task before Eve was created was to cultivate the garden and keep it. There was no need to give instructions about his headship as a husband because he had no wife at the time. It was after the temptation and the fall of man that God gave further instructions about the order and leadership of the union called marriage. Even to this day and time, I believe many Christian women have wondered, *Man of God, where are you?* when it comes to men's responsibilities. There have been a lot of responsibilities placed on the man; he is pulled in many directions and carries a lot on his shoulders. A lot is expected of him. He must provide for his home and family. In addition, his wife desires his love and time. He also is expected to be the family spiritual leader. With all these expectations, he very well may feel a need for space, go into his shell, and withdraw from what is demanded of him. Everyone is entitled to have some personal time out for refreshing, relaxation, and rest designed for the good; nevertheless, it should be taken without neglecting responsibilities. What is most important is that a man should be able to locate where he is, and know his role, his part, and his responsibility while seeking God's wisdom, along with the help of the Holy Spirit, to carry out his commission. God holds the man accountable for what he has been instructed to do, and for some reason, some men do not want to "man up," so to speak. To give further details about the fact that Adam had been given instructions concerning the tree of the knowledge of good and evil before Eve was created, we can see that Eve was very aware of the tree of good and evil, so evidently, she had been informed either by God or by Adam because she, in her conversation with the serpent, told him about the fruit of the tree that was in the midst of the garden. Not only was she knowledgeable of the tree of good and evil; she was influenced by the serpent to eat, and after she did partake and ate, she gave it to her husband, Adam, also to eat, which he did.

> And the woman said to the serpent, "We may eat the fruit of the trees of the garden; but of the fruit of the tree which is in the midst of the garden, God has said, "You shall not eat it, nor shall you touch it, lest you die." Then the serpent said to the woman, "You will not surely die. For God knows that in the day you eat of it your eyes will be opened, and you will be like God, knowing good and evil." So when the woman saw that the tree was good for food, that it was pleasant to the eyes, and a tree desirable to make one wise, she took of its fruit and ate. She also gave to her husband with her, and he ate.
>
> Genesis 3:2-6

Adam was there, and should have spoken up and put the serpent and the woman, Eve, in their places. He should have reminded them of the word of God, which said they were not to eat of this tree. Why did Adam not speak up? This was most definitely the time to declare what God had spoken, the time to take full responsibility for God's command. I wonder what Adam was thinking. Was he afraid to speak up, and was he so in love with his wife that he allowed her to have her way? Why did he eat the fruit instead of obeying God? If a wife is telling or acting out anything contrary to the Word of God, be it the written word of God or His spoken word by the Spirit of God, the husband is not to give in and comply with his wife. It is better to obey God than to sacrifice. Men, of course, you love your wives as Christ loved the church and give yourselves to them, in line with obedience and not contradiction to God. Jesus Christ was not in opposition with God, but He did the will of His Father. Men, you are to do likewise, no matter the cost. God holds you responsible, for He has crowned you with His glory. You are God's men and should not hide yourselves from the things of the Lord. Men of God, come out! Come out from wherever you may be hiding, and walk in that to which you are called. Let God arise and bring forth that wonderful mighty man of valor, for you are fearfully and wonderfully made.

When it comes to your wife, love her as you walk in the wisdom of God, and show understanding, along with consideration, of her. Your wife is your helpmate, and she desires to have balance in the marriage. She sometimes unknowingly really needs your leadership. One thing a wife does not like is feeling rejected by her husband. So somehow find a way to communicate with her using a love language so she can understand. As the husband in the marriage, your primary role is to love your wife as Christ loved the church—to provide for, protect, and dwell with her *with* understanding, and be not bitter with her.

My husband and I have had conversations about things that we have had differences about in our thinking. Differences in beliefs and opinions are universal in most marriages, friendships, coworker-and-employee relationships, parent-and-child relationships, politics, or any conversation between two people. It's common that people feel right concerning their viewpoint on how things should be. Every person is entitled to feel what he or she feels about things; after all, there is Scripture that says, "Every way of a man is right in his own eyes, but the Lord weighs the hearts" (Proverbs 21:2).

Because man is right in his own eyes, there is no guarantee two people will always see eye to eye on things. Even though it's okay to agree to disagree on certain subjects, agreeing on what is right and in line with the Word of God should be the objective for all. Occasionally, no one is right or wrong on an issue discussed, and it's okay to agree to disagree. You each may think that a different restaurant serves the best-tasting steak. Both of you are entitled to your preferences, and therefore, both are right. The question is, Who's going to surrender and fulfill the other's desire? I have heard my husband say that a man will do pretty much anything for his wife if she treats him right, speaks to him in the right manner, builds his ego, is sweet, is respectful, and believes in him. He has made comments that men are really quite simple. Husbands, when you give what you desire, it will come back to you. I responded that most Christian wives believe they are doing the right thing by their husbands respectfully, but there is something in the line of communication that does not seem to be understood.

Women will tell you what's in their hearts. They make it as plain and simple as it can be made, and yet men still do not get it. That baffles me. Mike, my husband, tells me women want to have things done their way, and if they are not getting their way, they tend to make things more challenging for their husbands. This action boomerangs, causing their husbands to take the stand of not giving in. Women want the control, Mike explains, and husbands are not giving it to them. Husbands sometimes will respond in a way that's not to their wives' liking. Husbands shut down, going into a shell that gives them shelter from their wives' emotions. In essence, husbands are in a stance of leadership, making the final decision, which may reflect an uncaring attitude toward the wife.

Over the years, with much communication with married women, I have encountered some who express how they have experienced responses from their loving husbands that made them feel, in the core of their soul, unloved. Husbands are expected to love their wives as Christ loved the church and gave Himself. If a wife does not truly have that sacrificial love from her husband, then the man of God is in hiding. God is love, and a husband loving his wife should be his foremost display. Understanding that their authority was delegated to them by God and that they have the final say, husbands should endeavor not to deprive their wives of their love. A husband should assure his wife by giving her the comfort of his love that is embedded in him to give, for in doing so, the husband will demonstrate that he is not in hiding, but in the character of God's man. Don't be one of those husbands who know what the Word says concerning wives' submitting to husbands, yet fail to do the Word of God when it comes to their obligation. If the wife is submitting to the husband and the husband is failing to submit to her, she is in obedience and the husband is not. The Bible, in Ephesians 5:21, says we should be "submitting to one another in the fear of God." A husband is responsible as the wife's head to love her like Christ loved the church, and if the wife is not seeing or feeling that love from you, as the husband, it's time to repent, get with the program, line yourself up, come out of hiding, and become a doer, and not just a hearer, of the Word of God. Husbands are warriors in the army of the Lord; therefore, they should be all that they are called to be in God's army. Man of God, where are you? Come out of hiding and man up! One, two, three, march, march, march, and take the lead to stride in the Word of God. You "can do all things through Christ who strengthens" you (Philippians 4:13). Purpose within your heart that you will be a doer of the Word of God. Stop looking at what you think, see, and feel; walk by faith and not by sight. Your wife is not called to be the man—you are. God's ways are higher than our ways, and He knows what's best for this union called marriage. Just think, He placed the husband as commander in chief, the leader; therefore, lead. Husbands, when you are in need of help, call on the Lord, and He will answer you.

> Call to Me, and I will answer you, and show you great and mighty things, which you do not know.
> Jeremiah 33:3

> I called on the Lord in distress; the Lord answered me and set me in a broad place.
> Psalm 118:5

> The Lord is near to all who call upon Him, to all who call upon Him in truth.
> Psalm 145:18

> Therefore I say to you, whatever things you ask when you pray, believe that you receive them, and you will have them.
> Mark 11:24

> And in that day you will ask Me nothing. Most assuredly, I say to you, whatever you ask the Father in My name He will give you. Until now you have asked nothing in My name. Ask, and you will receive, that your joy may be full.
> John 16:23-24

You, as a husband, must seek the Lord, and call on Him. Talk with Him, and ask Him for what you may need. He is there to assist you. He has already taken consideration of helping you by means of your wife—your helpmate to come alongside you. When was the last time you truly called on the name of the Lord concerning your marriage—or anything? God will hear your cry to Him. Call Him, for the Lord is our Helper. God is always there when you need Him. There are times when men perceive women are trying to gain control. An example is when an unmarried man is taking a woman out for dinner, or if a married man's wife is telling him to do something. He may be in the car driving, and she may suggest going in a certain direction as a shortcut. Refusing to do it, he continues to go his way. Maybe the wife asks her husband to turn the television on another channel just for a moment so she may view something quickly, assuring him that he can turn it right back, but he refuses to do it. Has your wife ever said something like, "Will you go to the store to pick up milk (or something else needed)?" or, "The children need their dad to spend time with them"? When a wife is giving her opinion or asking her husband to do something, she is not necessarily trying to gain control. Try looking at it from a different perspective, and see your wife's heart in the matter. She is only trying to help her husband or needs her husband to consider her. Remember, she is your helpmate; allow her to be what she is without being so quick to resist or criticize her help. When husbands know their wives' intention, it will help the husbands identify what really is going on. Women are known to be sensitive nurturers, and they should be respected and have their intentions considered, especially if they are not pointing out anything contrary to God's Word or standard. Your wife will know that you hear and consider her when you give her the same respect that you desire when you voice your opinions.

Husbands, it's good to love and care for your wives like they are good at the nurture of others. "Nurture" is a word that husbands also should take accountability for in the home, not looking at nurturing as something that should only come forth from the wives. If you are hiding in the area of nurture, come out of that hiding place, and give your wife the nurturing that she so needs from her husband. It's easy to find fault in others, but this question should be asked: Am I doing my part? Man of God, love your wife without making excuses because of how she may act. The husbands are accountable to do their part, and in doing so, they will see that their wives will respond positively to the love they receive. Women are receivers, and consequently, that which is given in word or deed to them to receive is deposited on the inside of them. And you may possibly have a withdrawal of what's within your wife. Keeping in mind that women are receivers and whatsoever the man sows, he shall reap, can help a husband gain that which he would want to receive in return or steer clear of what he doesn't want to gain.

If the wife has grown in maturity to the level communicated in the chapter "God's Man or My Man?" all of the husband's deposits are transferred in her heart's registry, now stamped "safe deposit," coupled with the words "submission with prayer."

Man of God, if the wife has not yet matured and is receiving from her husband negativity, disapproval, criticism, sarcasm, coldness, bitterness, indifference, a lack of appreciation, and irritability, she will respond to her husband negatively in return. On the other hand, if the wife receives from her husband positivity, approval, praise, kindness, warmth, sweetness, concern, appreciation, and an easygoing manner, the husband will have a positive response. As God's children, we are each responsible for doing our part, to seek our own soul salvation and be a doer of the Word according to the instructions given. A husband may feel it's difficult to give such loving care if the wife nags, is critical of her husband, is hard to please, and does not keep the house clean. Maybe your meals are not always prepared when you get home, or the children are not properly cared for according to the husband's standards. Loving your wife through it all is important, showing God and her that you are doing your part. Pray for her, and allow God to deal with her heart as well. You will get from her what you invest in her. She will love you when her husband *first* loves her. A wife will blossom in full when she is fulfilled. If a husband feels that his wife does not love him, he should ask himself this question: Have I loved her the way she needs to be loved, like Christ loved the church? The responsibility for a marriage to be successful primarily rests on the husband, the head, taking the initiative to love unselfishly. For the husband to love his wife like Christ loved the church, if he desires to follow Jesus in such a sacrificial denial of Himself ultimately to His death, the husband will have to get his own feelings out of the way. Displaying such a tremendous love as Jesus demonstrated requires one to deny himself or herself, take up one's own personal cross (which may be quite heavy), and follow Christ. Jesus did not hold anything back. He gave His all; He gave His life for the church.

A husband looking after and considering his wife, while cultivating love, should be a reflection seen in the marriage. The failure of the husband to do what needs to be done could cause the wife to get out of her submissive position and step up to the plate herself, so to speak. Once the roles are misconstrued and out of order, the confusion and mishaps will occur, causing each spouse to see that the other is not doing his or her part. As more conflict transpires, it leads to self-interest. Ultimately, selfishness on one or the other's part is what has caused many marriages to falter, collapse, and end in divorce. If both spouses can get their eyes off self- centeredness and on meeting the other's needs, both will have their desires given to them. Too many Christian men believe their role is completed as long as they are bringing home the bacon, not realizing there is more involved in providing for the family, especially where the wife is concerned. Christ loved the church sacrificially and unconditionally; likewise, husbands, let not your love for your wife be in hiding, but an open love that manifests and identifies the same as Christ's unconditional sacrifice.

Man of God, when your wife asks you a question or has a request, she should not be given an abrupt, callous, insensitive response compared with when someone else asks the very same question or makes the same request. Are your responses respectful, smooth, and at times given with a smiling face when it's others whom you are talking with, but not so with your wife? What makes the difference? Why is there more respect given to others than to wives? There are husbands who open doors for other women without giving their wives the same courtesy. Why? It's a good question to ask if the husband has ever found himself in this predicament. I ask this because apparently, some husbands are more respectful to others than to their own wives. The wife feels it when her husband is manifesting his aggravation toward her, especially in the company of others. Perhaps there's a communication gap that needs to be understood and filled. At times during a conversation between a husband and a wife, the husband may say something like, "I don't understand." Understanding is something the Bible requires a husband to dwell in with his wife. For one not to understand something that is told to him or her shows that the person does not have the knowledge of what was spoken.

In the next chapter, I will show ways to clearly express to your wife that you are in understanding. Women do not believe they are speaking a foreign language or some educated philosophy beyond the intellectual capacity of their husbands. To women, they are making it as plain and simple as they can with a clarity that anyone should be able to understand. This may be the reason wives are perplexed when husbands respond with, "I don't understand." She may even feel resentment. She wonders, *How can my husband not understand what to me I am clearly expressing?* Man of God, where are you? Come out of hiding, rise up to what's happening, and rescue and assure her that you understand her. Loving her symbolically as Christ loved the church is also being a refuge, a safe haven, for her. Instead of being in hiding, you can become that hiding place of consolation for her to come to whenever she needs her husband. Jesus Christ is always there for the church. He is the church's Head; likewise, the husband, as the head of the wife, is to be there for her. The man of God is made in the image of God; he is God's creation, and because the man is in God's divine order of authority, his say carries a lot of weight. As an example, in Genesis chapter 27, read how Rebekah knew and understood the value of her husband, Isaac's speaking words of blessing over their son. She deliberately went as far as tricking her husband to attain his words of blessing for Jacob, the youngest son. Isaac was about to bless the elder son, Esau, so Rebekah manipulated a plan whereby Jacob would receive the blessing through the words that were about to come forth from her husband. She knew her husband's words were as good as gold and a done deal once spoken, that if he said it, it was so! She knew that God would honor her husband's words, and she willingly went about trickery to get him to speak his blessings over Jacob. Man of God, be cautious of what you say or how you speak to your wife or your children. Words are powerful, and as a result, the wife will take them to heart and be unmistakably affected by them, good or bad. Husbands are the heads, the chiefs, in the households, the ones set in authority, and what the husbands verbalize is unquestionably powerful.

Furthermore, prayers can be hindered because of bitterness. I find it attention-grabbing that in the Word of God, husbands are instructed to love their wives, rather than be bitter toward them.

> Husbands, love your wives and do not be bitter toward them.
>
> Colossians 3:19

We know as new creations in Christ Jesus, we all are to walk in love, and in marriage, husbands are told to love their wives. The apostle Paul is indicating that husbands stay on the side of love. He made the statement in the above text because he must have known there is a tendency for husbands to sometimes be bitter toward their wives. There is quite a contrast between two words Paul chose to speak, **love** and **bitter**.

First, expounding on the word **bitter**. A husband must be watchful that bitterness does not exist in his heart toward his wife, for out of the abundance of the heart the mouth speaks. If there is bitterness within his heart, it is identified because it will come out of his mouth. If bitterness exists, it's good to get rid of it. Let's consider the word **"bitter"** by imagining a tart, harsh, and unpleasant taste inside the mouth. Get that? Inside the mouth! A person usually doesn't recognize that something is bitter unless it's first put into the mouth, tasted, and sensed by the tongue. What's in a man will come out, and if bitterness is hidden inside a person, it conceivably will manifest itself in an outward appearance in many ways that are apparent to the physical eye. It can be a bitter, insensitive word filtering from the heart, releasing from the mouth, and bringing forth resentment, anger, animosity, hostility, and an unpleasantly sour taste. After tasting something that is **bitter**, we may be quick to frown, showing our disapproval with an unpleasant facial expression.

Because of the unpleasant taste, we may spew it out of our mouth. On the tongue are taste buds that are capable of recognizing four basic kinds of tastes, namely sweet, salty, sour, and **bitter**. So we can, without hesitation, say that all four are identified and stored up in the mouth, and that the stronger ones manifest in what comes out of the mouth by way of words. This indicates how powerful words are for everyone involved. Of the taste buds, there is only one kind that is more engaging and favorable to all people, and that is the sweet taste bud. Everybody enjoys sweets, even if he or she doesn't eat a lot of them. People enjoy something sweet, even if it's only fruit. Salty, sour, and **bitter** are not tastes that all people like. Sweet words are lovable words. In the chapter "God's Man or My Man?" I illustrated to the wife how her behavior, not her words, is what will win over her husband. Everyone is held accountable for words that are spoken. There is power in spoken words. Men, I have conveyed the importance of how husbands speak to their wives with the hope of demonstrating as well as enlightening your understanding so you can be acquainted with the word **"bitter"** and not allow it near your wives.

Death and life are in the power of the tongue, and those who love it will eat its fruit.

Proverbs 18:21

A good man out of the good treasure of his heart brings forth good things, and an evil man out of the evil treasure brings forth evil things. But I say to you that for every idle word men may speak, they will give account of it in the day of judgment. For by your words you will be justified, and by your words you will be condemned.

Matthew 12:35-37

Jesus speaks a parable to the disciples: It's not what goes into the mouth that defiles a man, but what comes out of the mouth that defiles a man. Peter asked Jesus to explain this parable of defilement that Jesus spoke of, so He did, saying:

> ...Are you also still without understanding? Do you not yet understand that whatever enters the mouth goes into the stomach and is eliminated? But those things which proceed out of the mouth come from the heart, and they defile a man. For out of the heart proceed evil thoughts, murders, adulteries, fornications, thefts, false witness, blasphemies. These are the things which defile a man, but to eat with unwashed hands does not defile a man.
>
> Matthew 15:16-20

Lord, help us all to speak words of **love**, words that will edify and build up and not tear down. Husbands, choose the side of **love** and not **bitterness** toward your wives. When you **love** your wife, you are not allowing **bitterness** or resentment through nonverbal actions that show you are irritated with her. Are there any husbands manifesting anger, animosity, hostility, or unpleasantness at things their wives do? Spending time in prayer will give an attitude adjustment if this is something that has been lingering for some time. Do not let the sun go down on your wrath; exercise the **love** walk. **Love** is the key word! **Love** never fails. **Love** your wife as Christ loved the church and "gave" Himself for it. Jesus did not wait until the church loved Him before He gave Himself. Nor did God wait until the world first loved Him before He gave His only begotten Son. No! They loved first and then gave, regardless of what they received in return. The world had turned its back on God, and people spat on His Son, Jesus, yet they purposely walked in **love**.

As a husband, do you pout and wait for your wife to **love** first before you show **love** toward her? No! Husbands, go first, and the wives will follow the heads. Notice that a head is set at the top, the first part of the body, the beginning. The head is not set at the center of the body, nor was it placed at the lower part of the body where the feet are. The husband, the head, is not to be self-centered and waiting to be served, but in service toward his wife, who is a part of his body. "So husbands ought to love their own wives as their own bodies; he who loves his wife loves himself" (Ephesians 5:28). Jesus Christ paid His price for the church. He was your perfect Role Model, and what did He do? He gave Himself. Man of God, you have been instructed to **"love"** your wife and not be **bitter** toward her. Ephesians 5:25 says, "Husbands, love your wives, just as Christ also loved the church and gave Himself for her." Husbands are to **love** their wives. I make mention of this a lot because I want husbands to really get it. In the marriage union, the men have specifically been told to **love** their wives. Why? Wives really do need **love,** and husbands are to give it to their wives. Set the example as Christ did. If husbands were not capable of doing so, they would not have been instructed to do so. As a husband, if your love has been in hiding, bring it out, for it's required. Husbands are to feel affection in favor of their wives. Adore her, and stop blaming her for what you may not be doing. Don't wait or hesitate, but do unto her as you would have done unto you. She is not an excuse, a scapegoat for the lack of responsibility. If a husband is not feeling this **love** toward his wife, I recommend praying for it to be restored. Faith can be exercised by starting with loving the wife and removing any bitterness from the mouth toward her. Overpower the bitterness, and replace it with the sweetness that also resides within the mouth. It may have been one of the four tastes lying dormant, but it's there. Try it; it's sweet!

Pleasant words are like a honeycomb, sweetness
to the soul and health to the bones.

Proverbs 16:24

The husband is responsible for what goes on in the
household—how he treats his wife, regardless of her
actions, and doing his part—because God will hold him
accountable in carrying out instructions delegated to
him. Can the rest of the body function without its head?
Absolutely not! Can the body get up and go to the mailbox
to get the mail on its own, leaving the head behind? The
very thought of going to the mailbox will first come from
the head, and then the body will respond by lining up
in cooperation with the thought from the head, and the
body will get up and go get the mail from the mailbox.
The body cannot do anything of itself without the head
leading it. It's impossible to live a productive life without
the head functioning properly. Do you see that the husband as the head really is an important role that affects
the outcome of the body? Better yet, the body will be
undeveloped without the leading of the head. Whenever
the head is functioning properly, the entire body and
everything that is governed by it will follow its leading
with a flow, bringing all parts in harmony with one
another. The man of God reigning in his fullness will
not be in hiding in any area that God has called him to
be in. Christ is the Head of every man, whether he is a
single or married man.

But I want you to know that the head of every
man is Christ, the head of woman is man, and the
head of Christ is God.

1 Corinthians 11:3

There are no exceptions to man's having headship.
The apostle Paul wants us to know that Christ is the
Head of every man. No one is left without a head to

answer to—not the man, not the woman, not Christ Jesus, for each has a head, and with each head comes responsibility. This verse does not indicate that the woman is in headship. She does not have this responsibility, but every man does. The word "every" says it all. Sometimes men can put themselves in the category of professional relaxers. When they are not working on the job, most of their time is consumed by things that relax them, such as television, sports, fishing, lying in a hammock, and more sports. It's okay to wind down and loosen up, but in all that you do, remember the wife and the children, remember who you are and what you were called to do, and remember the head leads on the pathway. Remember that a body cannot function without its head, and remember YOU are the head. Not some, but all, husbands are heads of their wives; therefore, as a husband, stand in your position of loving her like Christ loved the church by doing your part. Should the husband want to go in a shell and hide, a safe hiding place is in Christ Jesus, your Refuge, YOUR Head.

The test: Taking the responsibility as a husband of answering the call of duty and not being in hiding.

The trial: The man of God in quality as a husband to his wife as ordained by God.

The testimony: Husbands are no longer in hiding, but in obedience, submitting to the Word of God and loving their wives as Christ loved the church. Husbands are giving their wives the love they deserve without walking in bitterness toward them. In return, husbands will have happy wives, happy lives, and happy home environments, as they walk in the fruit of love.

Pray this prayer: *Father, You said to acknowledge You in all my ways, and You will direct my path. Holy Spirit,* *help me as I endeavor to love my wife as Christ loved the church and give myself to her. As her covering, I will protect, watch over, and love my wife with sweet and kind words, removing any bitterness that may try to manifest itself. I recognize that Christ is my Head and that I will answer to Him. Help me, Father, to not hide myself from the beauty of holiness in being the man of God that You have ordained me to be in my home. Thank You, heavenly Father, in advance for all that You are doing in and through me, that all may see Christ through me and glorify Your name. In Jesus' name I pray. Amen.*

Dwelling With Your Wife With Understanding

> Husbands, likewise, dwell with them with understanding, giving honor to the wife, as to the weaker vessel, and as being heirs together of the grace of life, that your prayers may not be hindered.
>
> 1 Peter 3:7

To "dwell" is to reside, inhabit, and make your home in. For a husband to dwell with his wife with understanding means that he is thinking of her and taking her into consideration by showing kindness toward her and appreciation of her. It is well-known that at times men have said they do not understand their wives. With all due respect, it is your responsibility, as a husband, to dwell, or live, with her with understanding. Ask the Holy Spirit to help you, and research suggestions. Many resources exist that will educate you on a woman's philosophy. There is a great deal of knowledge available to help you dwell with her with understanding, so it would be wise to go after it and "get it."

> Wisdom is the principal thing; therefore get wisdom. And in all your getting, get understanding.
>
> Proverbs 4:7

Here we see that "wisdom is the principal thing." Wisdom is the truth that is the foundation of getting understanding. Solomon was one who had wisdom with a deep understanding of people. Wisdom is a deep understanding and realizing of people, things, events, or situations, resulting in the ability to choose or act to consistently produce the optimum results with minimal time and energy. Wisdom is the quality or state of being wise; knowledge of what is true or right coupled with just judgment as to action; sagacity, discernment, or insight.

When we read the book of Proverbs, we find many Scriptures that show wisdom and understanding flowing alongside each other. To get one is to go after and get the other. I love the fact that wisdom is described as a female. This may help you understand why women think they know everything. Although they don't know everything, there's a lot of wisdom in most women. Let's look at more Scriptures related to wisdom, and for your understanding, think of how they may relate to your wife as you read them.

> Happy is the man who finds wisdom, and the man who gains understanding; for her proceeds are better than the profits of silver, and her gain than fine gold. She is more precious than rubies, and all the things you may desire cannot compare with her. Length of days is in her right hand, in her left hand riches and honor. Her ways are ways of pleasantness, and all her paths are peace. She is a tree of life to those who take hold of her, and happy are all who retain her.
>
> Proverbs 3:13-18

> For whoever finds me finds life, and obtains favor from the Lord.
>
> Proverbs 8:35

He who finds a wife finds a good thing, and obtains favor from the Lord.

Proverbs 18:22

Wisdom has built her house, she has hewn out her seven pillars.

Proverbs 9:1

The wise woman builds her house, but the foolish pulls it down with her hands.

Proverbs 14:1

Having a wise woman as a wife should give you the security of knowing that what matters to her is building her house. She will not be foolish and pull it down with her hands. Your wife wants the best for the two of you in the marriage. She is acquainted with wisdom and understanding, and has a perception of how best things should go. I like the fact that "wisdom" is referred to as "her" and "she," meaning female. Your wife has perception when it comes to wisdom. So humble yourself at times, and ask her advice on some things; she could be good counsel for you. You married her; she is your trusted companion. The sooner a husband comes to the realization that his wife is there to help, to do him good and not harm, the sooner he can comfortably go to her and ask for her advice on a matter. Asking for your wife's counsel or advice is not allowing her to make the decisions, but just checking with her to see if your evaluation is correct. Lay down pride, and ask her. You may be surprised at her wisdom. Are you ready to listen and consider her viewpoint?

Once I heard a well-known pastor on a radio station telling men that it pays for them to listen to their wives. Your wife really does have insight and knows some things you can learn. Husbands should yearn to understand their wives as part of loving them. "A fool has no delight in understanding, but in expressing his own heart" (Proverbs 18:2). The opposite of this is to find pleasure and enjoyment in understanding, and then you will not be a fool.

It seems safe to say that if you are not dwelling with your wife with understanding and following the instructions in the Bible, your prayers will be hindered. To dwell with your wife with understanding, knowledge is required, so you may have to do some studying. Study your wife, and find out what she really needs. What makes her happy? What makes her miserable or sad? What makes her comfortable and at ease? What makes her beam with a smile? What makes her joyful? What makes her pleasant? What makes her feel loved? Purchase some good Christian books that will help you understand her. These are good things to know to help you dwell with your wife with understanding. Ask her about herself, and then listen to her. More than likely, she is willing to tell you how she feels. Don't reject what she says, but "look, listen, learn," and be there for her. That is more valuable than all the material things you may provide. When she is given your undivided attention, it shows your sense of obligation toward her. Sometimes she just needs to talk, without your feeling that you have to solve anything. Giving your ear as she pours out her heart is showing your desire to understand her. She feels secure when she knows she can freely release what's going on inside her.

To further clarify the importance of the married man's honoring his wife, let's read from the Amplified Bible about the connection between the effectiveness of your prayers and how you treat your wife.

In the same way you married men should live considerately with [your wives], with an intelligent recognition [of the marriage relation], honoring the woman as [physically] the weaker, but [realizing that you] are joint heirs of the grace (God's unmerited favor) of life, in order that your prayers may not be hindered and cut off. [Otherwise you cannot pray effectively.]

1 Peter 3:7 AMP

The outcome of your prayers is dependent upon how considerate you are of your wife. People tend to honor, protect, and cherish that which they consider precious. If you prize your wife as being most precious to you, you will give her what's due her.

When men say to their wives that the men do not understand, is it sometimes just an excuse to get out of a conversation or responsibility? Could it be that they understand what they want to understand? Or do they really not understand? If the latter is true, the solution would be to go after and get understanding. Seek it out, and you will find it. What's baffling is that it appears men understand most subjects that are commonly discussed until they feel a sense of obligation. There appears to be a blockage when in conversation, they feel a pull, an expectation that something is required or that they have a responsibility, especially if they do not want to do something.

Expounding on the word "understanding" in the quoted text, I will bring forth a number of other words of expression that will help you see more clearly the very words that are important to your wife and what she desires from you. Understanding your wife is manifested when you are **considerate**. How can you be **considerate**? You can show her you are being **considerate** of her through **thoughtfulness** by helping with chores, taking some of the load off of her. It may mean spending quality time with her alone and also quality time alone with the children. Listen to her when she tells you how she feels without turning things around and blaming her. That is not the time to do that. Men can be masters at turning things around, finding fault in the women while they're talking. But that only shows that you, as the husband, are not taking responsibility. When your wife is expressing herself to you, it's your time to listen and **consider** her feelings, not afflict her more through your criticism. Listen and nod your head up and down as if you agree and understand (even if you don't at the time). In addition, this is a great opportunity for you to comfort her, hold her, and assure her of your love.

Showing her that you **appreciate** her also tells her you are being **considerate**. Doing so will say to her that you are pleased with her, and you recognize that she desires time with you and you are willing to give her just that. Your actions speak louder than your words, so don't ignore her. If you do, she will eventually back down, and you, too, will be ignored. The love factor totally depends on your giving love. Your wife loves you, and spending time with her and the children assures her of your love for the family. If you do otherwise, you might as well say she does not deserve your sacrificial love. When you are **thoughtful**, you show **kindness**, **acceptance**, **indulgence**, **perception**, **sensitivity** **sympathy**, **appreciation**, **gratefulness**, and **support**. Although your wife is your helpmate, she also needs *your* help and *your* **tolerance**—your being open-minded enough to realize she needs you to put up with her as well as she puts up with you.

The preceding words written in boldface give you full knowledge so you may comprehend what your wife desires from you. Surprisingly, each of the bold words above is a synonym for the word **"understanding"**— imagine that! The word has told you to dwell with your wife with understanding. So it would be fair to say that you are to dwell with her with each of the words printed in bold above—that's it, in a nutshell—and then you will be dwelling with your wife with understanding. She will see you as the unselfish man of God that you are ordained to be.

In most marriages, women are expressing their hearts, telling their husbands what they think or feel. Your wife may question why something she told you is so challenging for you to understand. Why is that? Is it being rebellious? If so, you know that rebellion is not of God. It is as the sin of witchcraft, and you don't want to open up that door. Ask yourself, do you feel you are in authority only when you are having the final say? Doing your part does not take away from your authority. It only *shows* that you have authority, for you are the one making the decision to love your wife the way Christ loves the church. Remember, Christ died for us. He "gave" His life, and it did not take anything away from His authority. Jesus Christ, in obedience to the cross, was the One in victory. To whom much is given, much is required. Your rank in authority requires your love; it requires you to dwell with your wife with understanding.

> For God so loved the world that He *gave* His only begotten Son, that whoever believes in Him should not perish but have everlasting life.
>   John 3:16 (emphasis added)

God loved the world so much that He "gave" His Son, Christ Jesus, who also "gave" His life. Husbands, too, are commissioned to "give" of themselves to their wives. You, as a husband, are the one set in command, the one leading, required to follow God and the Son's example of their love. When you make a declaration to whose side you are on, you can cause things to sway one way or the other. Choose to be obedient to the Word of God. Just as with the wife, a lot falls on your lot. We all pay a price in following the love of God. It is commanded of you, as the husband, a warrior, to love your wife as Christ loved the church. You are strong in the Lord, and through seeking God's face and guidance, you will be kept in all your ways. Your wife is not ruling you when you give in to some of her desires. There has been no change of position. You are not a wimp, nor are you henpecked because you demonstrate love toward your wife. According to the Word of God, you are simply putting into practice what you were instructed to do.

> For the husband is head of the wife, as also Christ is head of the church; and He is the Savior of the body.
>
> Ephesians 5:23

In this verse, we read that the husband is the head of the wife. The head leads; it's the top part of the body, which directs the body's flow. As the husband, you are your wife's covering and protection. What she desires, you are to provide. Jesus Christ did not oppress, overlook, tyrannize, or bully the church around. Jesus Christ sacrificially and unselfishly gave Himself, that we may live. Being the one in authority does not imply that a husband is to treat his wife as a doormat, placing his feet on her and keeping her down. No! You, as a husband, are, according to the Scriptures, commanded to love your wife.

> Husbands, love your wives, just as Christ also loved the church and gave Himself for her, that He might sanctify and cleanse her with the washing of water by the word, that He might present her to Himself a glorious church, not having spot or wrinkle or any such thing, but that she should be holy and without blemish. So husbands ought to love their own wives as their own bodies; he who loves his wife loves himself. For no one ever hated his own flesh, but nourishes and cherishes it, just as the Lord does the church. . . . "For this reason

a man shall leave his father and mother and be joined to his wife, and the two shall become one flesh."

Ephesians 5:25-29, 31

We know that Christ loved the church sacrificially and unconditionally. Many times men want to be served, but ask yourself how many times you have served your wife. Jesus did not come to be served, but to serve. Men want respect, yet some do not show respect to their wives. Do you respect your wife as you want to be respected? Do you listen to her and respect her at home as well as in the company of others, not embarrassing, shaming, or putting her down so that she doesn't feel important to you? Are you ever sarcastic and scornful toward your wife? If so, stop it! It only shows you are haughty and self-important in character. You see her; you see a reflection of yourself. Treat her the way you would like to be treated. Do you love yourself? Love her as well.

God has ordained you to be in authority, or in leadership of your wife. For Eve was created right out of Adam, made from his innermost part, one of your ribs. To not do right by your wife is to not do right by yourself. You are to love her like you do your own body, for she is a portion of you. To the point, listen to the words the first man said:

Adam said: "This is now bone of my bones and flesh of my flesh; she shall be called Woman, because she was taken out of Man."

Genesis 2:23

Adam was emphasizing that his wife was a portion of him, and when he loved his wife, he loved his own flesh. In a nutshell, Eve was Adam, and so is your wife YOU! You are one. We can read the association of what

Adam said also in the New Testament, which gives further details as to how a husband should love his "own" wife as his own body, not someone else's wife or any other woman.

> So husbands ought to love their own wives as their own bodies; he who loves his wife loves himself. For no one ever hated his own flesh, but nourishes and cherishes it, just as the Lord does the church.
>
> Ephesians 5:28-29

With the hope of shedding more light and understanding on the husband's duties, I'm going to pull from the above text two key words: **"nourishes"** and **"cherishes."** As I expound on these words, know that Jesus Christ also loved His body, which is the church:

> And He put all things under His feet, and gave Him to be head over all things to the church, which is His body, the fullness of Him who fills all in all.
>
> Ephesians 1:22-23

His body is the church, which He, too, honors as His most valuable part, and not even the gates of hell can prevail against it. So let it be with husbands toward their wives. A husband should protect his wife and his marriage, and not allow anything or anyone to separate him from his love for his wife. When the wife knows the depth of her husband's love and feels secure in her marriage, she is assured of his commitment, and most likely she will, with pleasure, submit to her husband and follow his leadership, his example of being Christlike.

Christ, in fact, **nourishes** the church. He made sure the church did not suffer from a lack of **nourishment** of the Word of God, so that we are cleansed and grow by it. He did not leave the church to die from spiritual malnutrition. Christ feeds the church what it needs to grow so that He might present to Himself a glorious church, not having a spot or wrinkle or any such thing, so that she is holy and without blemish. Jesus gave us the Holy Ghost to be our Comforter, and to teach, lead, and guide us. As a husband, you are to do likewise with your wife; that is, tend to her growing, take care of her, and keep her alive and well. Feed, nurture, protect, and comfort her. Take care of her by making provision, and yes, although she is your helpmate, you, too, can help her with **nourishment** and support.

Take a glance at the beginning of time. Adam's first responsibility was to tend and cultivate the land. You, too, are a cultivator, one who can cause growth. I know you may be thinking, *More work!* Actually, the work of **nourishing** your wife is really quite simple. Realizing that you are already working and providing income to the household and feeding your wife (and any children) says you are providing some **nourishment**. Extra **nourishment** can be supplied through giving your wife compliments and showing appreciation of what she does around the house and for your children. Take her out on dates, and make quality time just for talks with her alone. Go for joyrides in the car. Encourage her in things she sets out to do. How about frequently affirming your love for her? Have some quiet times together, such as reading a chapter in the Bible together and praying in agreement on family and church matters. You might watch a movie of her choice, or watch a Christian television program together. Sometimes simply saying to her, "Thank you" or "I appreciate you" gives merit. Implementing some or all of these periodically will go a long way toward causing her to feel your love, approval, and admiration, and will give her the pleasure of feeling alive, well, full, and satisfied. Aaahhh, **nourishment**! It does the wife good. It makes her soul feel relaxed, secure, safe, and satisfied to have her doses of nourishment provided.

Putting forth effort in this area more often than usual will give you lots of brownie points with your wife, and show her that you have her best interests at heart. It's a known fact that **nourishment** is good for the body; without it, the body will be malnourished and vulnerable to disease and starvation. Anything you feed will grow. If it is not fed, it will starve and die. Therefore, feed the body, your wife, and your marriage, keeping all healthy and strong. Being the man of God that you are called to be takes an absolute love for God and your wife to the point that you are willing to give yourself totally, even unto death. Your wife is a portion of your own body; she is one with you. Your wife needs **nourishment**, just as your own body needs **nourishment**, and in order to have a healthy body (the two of you), it's important that it does not suffer any lack; therefore, **nourish** your wife in what's suitable for her. Doing so reflects as well as demonstrates your love for your wife and also yourself! Scripture states:

> So husbands ought to love their own wives as their own bodies; he who loves his wife loves himself.
> Ephesians 5:28

Do you love your own body? If you love your own body, you will love her as well. Coming to our second keyword and identifying with what the Lord did for the church, you are to **cherish** your wife, to hold her dear and treat her with tenderness and not with harshness. You are to treasure and watch over her with loving care in addition to having affection for her. So what are some ways that you can show her she is **cherished**? Show her she is valuable in your relationship and that she is of great significance and worthy of your labor of love. Consideration as the weaker vessel takes a great weight off her shoulders. When you are bearing in mind her concerns, assuring her that you are there for her to lift the burden, it shows that you are sensitive to her worth; this happens every time you are being considerate, thoughtful, and kind toward her.

A Christian wife who looks to the Lord God for her spiritual strength also is inclined to look to her husband for strength in the physical state of being, which includes her mind, willpower, and emotions. For this reason, in the physical, the wife is considered the weaker vessel.

> Husbands, likewise, dwell with them with understanding, giving honor to the wife, as to the weaker vessel, and as being heirs together of the grace of life, that your prayers may not be hindered.
>
> 1 Peter 3:7

> And those [parts] of the body which we consider rather ignoble are [the very parts] which we invest with additional honor, and our unseemly parts and those unsuitable for exposure are treated with seemliness (modesty and decorum).
>
> 1 Corinthians 12:23 AMP

First Corinthians 12:23 from the Amplified Bible not only speaks to the collective body of Christ in unity, but also helps to broaden the understanding of 1 Peter 3:7, a Scripture concerning husbands giving honor to their wives as the weaker vessel. A wife is a part of the body of her husband. The very part (the wife) that is considered weaker is the very part (the wife) to invest with additional honor. WOW! She is quite special, and it takes a self-sacrificing act of love to invest "additional" honor. As the church has a need for Christ's love, it is evident that the wife needs her husband's love. If it were not important, it would not have been written in the

Scriptures. Husbands who model Christ's love in their marriage will find they have remarkable achievement. The head functioning properly determines the way to lead the entire body in the pathway of righteousness for the good of it.

Most married women are very aware that the husband in the home makes the chief decisions, yet they wait for him to man up to his call. When there is love and consideration of her, it will be evident for all to see through the radiance in her countenance that confirms that her husband is dwelling with her with understanding. Giving himself to her is an unselfish act, showing that the husband trusts God to make the provision he needs in order to provide for his wife. If a husband feels he doesn't know what to do to make his wife happy, this is another wonderful time to pray. Jesus specifically tells us, *". . . men always ought to pray and not lose heart"* (Luke 18:1). Men are in leadership, and God will listen to the heart of any leader. Why? God ordained authority, and any authority coming to Him, I believe, gets His attention. People are under authority everywhere, and God knows that He is their answer, and when the head gets straight in the stance of righteousness, the body can follow the leader's influence.

Sometimes a wife's demeanor may show evidence of a strong persona, yet she cries or shows a vulnerable side that may cause her husband not to understand. But as the leader and head, a husband is to dwell with her with understanding, and be kind, thoughtful, and considerate of her, not act as if he doesn't care. A wife needs her husband, for he is like Abraham was to Sarah, who called him her lord. A husband is his wife's strength, her rock, and her strong shoulder to lean on. He is her refuge, a safe haven, her protection. Given these character traits, men should, at this point, notice the fact that they're Christlike. Now can you understand the wife's need for you and your love? Can you now understand this is expected of you? You have the ability to create the situation in marriage that you both would love to have. A wife needs to feel that she is able to come to her husband for comfort when she needs it. A husband should not always expect her to be strong, or criticize her when she is frail. He is to consider and honor her as the weaker vessel. If she has an emotional moment with tears, as her husband, try putting your arms around her and giving her comfort and support, instead of walking away as if you are not concerned. Show her that you are being sensitive to her emotions. (Sensitivity toward your wife will not rob you of your manhood, but will demonstrate understanding to her.) Showing warmth, compassion, and kindness toward her is the same as cuddling with her. The word **"cherish"** primarily means "to hold dear, feel or show affection for. Adore, love, to keep and cultivate with care and affection.

Most wives like it when you cuddle with them, embrace them, hug them, and hold them. These things define the word **"cherish"** and maintain what is expected of you in your marriage.

Nourishing and **cherishing** your wife illustrates you are activating the Word of God in your marriage. Isn't it interesting that you are to give her these two things she craves? If this is something that is lacking, subsequently, you will be in a hidden place in your marriage and should ask yourself, Am I dwelling with my wife with understanding?

Another attribute for loving your wife just as Christ loved the church pertains to how you present her.

> ...that He might sanctify and cleanse her with the washing of water by the word, that He might present her to Himself a glorious church, not having spot or wrinkle or any such thing, but that she should be holy and without blemish.
>
> Ephesians 5:27

Stop for a moment and visualize the power, the authority of this verse. How a husband treats his wife is a reflection of his presentation of her to the Lord. How he treats her shows how he manages and takes care of her. I am not saying that a husband's wife is to have her way in everything, but it's pretty close to it, and will most definitely show God and others how she has been treated. Husbands are the leaders in the love walk to set the example of love. Husbands are expected to do so even if wives are the ones who are more apt to affection. Have a readiness to always be in pursuit of her. It's good to keep in mind that because of her, you not only have found a good thing, but you also have obtained favor from the Lord:

> He who finds a wife finds a good thing, and obtains favor from the Lord.
>
> Proverbs 18:22

To obtain favor from the Lord is to have His acts of kindness in your life. That in itself is a treasure worth having. How unselfish is it when a husband is providing for his wife's needs day after day, giving of his energy and strength? It is easy to understand why God will give him favor. He has been placed in a position of responsibility. To properly function, his wife's fulfillment and happiness must be more important than his own happiness. My, my, my, only a love like this can come from the Lord; therefore, all can understand the admiration and respect due to a husband who is expected to do likewise and love his wife.

The more a husband learns to love by example, the more his leadership is enhanced. He will be leading by his love walk. Faith works by love! Both are words of action. It is not words only, but deeds that get things accomplished. To say, "I love you" is good, and a wife would love to hear her husband tell her so, but without the actions to back up those words, the words will become meaningless to her. She needs you to show her through your actions that you love and understand her. Remember God's actions related to love? "For God so loved the world that He *gave* His only begotten Son" . . . and Jesus, the Son, *gave* of Himself. The actions of God and Jesus expressed an unconditional love toward the people they loved. Being a doer, not just a hearer, of the Word gets the assignment done.

To help you achieve success in loving your wife, let me give you a few words that are easy to remember so you can put them into practice as you are dwelling with your wife with understanding. I like to call them "the three C's": **comfort, cover, and cuddle.**

Comfort: Soothe, console, reassure, calm, ease, and relieve her of grief or sorrow, pacifying and replacing negative feelings or emotions or burdens with satisfaction and relief that everything will be all right. Restore her back to a cheerful heart.

Cover: Wrap your arms around her to give a feel of protection and warmth, causing her to be sheltered from anything that's trying to attack her, concealing her from any hurt, harm, or danger, whether physical or mental. Cover her with your prayers, and watch over her.

Cuddle: Hug, embrace, and hold her to show affection and kindness. These actions also give warmth and reassurance of a safe place. She will feel accepted in the arms of strength, held with gentleness.

If you implement these three C's and don't hold back because of any negativity you may be picking up from her, she will love you more. Women respond to what they are receiving, so continue to reassure her of your love for her. If she is a fighter and strongly resists, pray for God's help. You may have to give her some time; however, come at another time to embrace her. She will give in to your embrace, so don't give up and quit. She needs you more when she appears withdrawn; this is your signal to draw closer to her and not draw back.

One last word of encouragement: It's okay to listen to your wife as long as she is not outside the commandments, in disobedience to God. She usually is very sensitive and keenly aware. She could possibly "help" you to not become entangled in whatever you are dealing with in life.

The test: Husbands dwelling with understanding their wives.

The trial: Husbands overcoming selfishness and applying knowledge that helps them while dwelling with their wives with understanding.

The testimony: A husband presents his wife as blameless and without a spot or wrinkle to God, having been victorious in dwelling with his wife with understanding, pleasing God and obtaining favor with Him and man. The husband will gain confidence in who he is in the marriage, and have a satisfied wife.

Pray this prayer: *Father, I ask You to help me be the man that You have called me to be in dwelling with my wife with understanding. When I miss it, help me to not be prideful, but submit and align myself with the Word of God in obedience. I ask You, in Jesus' name, to help me as I love my wife as Christ loved the church and give myself to her. I will trust You with all my heart and lean not to my understanding, but in all my ways, I will acknowledge You. I pray that I overcome my own self-will. I look at and take time to study my wife and her needs. I ask for wisdom as I take on my responsibility of being a doer of Your Word. Father, I also ask You to remind me of the three C's, so that I may apply them in my marriage. I know my position and who I am in Christ*

Jesus, and I willingly give of myself in being an example in leading in the love walk. The Lord is my Helper, and I will do according to Your Word. Thank You, Father, for all that I ask, I believe that I have received in Jesus' name. Amen.

I DO

Therefore a man shall leave his father and mother
and be joined to his wife, and they shall become
one flesh.

Genesis 2:24

*Author's note: This chapter is especially for the benefit of
newlyweds; however, everyone can benefit from reading
it.*

You have recently said, "I do," making a vow in a
marriage union. Now you are living together with
someone you really thought you knew. Now there's
another person in the home besides you. Traditionally,
when you say, "I do," it's the female's last name that
changes. The man's name stays the same, but he gains
the responsibility of taking care of another person. You
may even ask yourself, *Who is this person I have wed
who now sleeps in my bed?* Oh, my! You are no longer
alone; this new life is made of two joined together pro-
gressively becoming one. God did not say that Adam
and Eve were one, but that they shall *become* one flesh.
Jesus reminds the disciples what God said when He
said, ". . . and the two shall become one flesh; so then
they are no longer two, but one flesh" (Mark 10:8).
"Becoming" implies that you will develop into one. There
will be times in your marriage when you will literally have

the same thoughts. For instance, you may be thinking of having pizza for dinner, and later you will hear your spouse say, "I thought about having pizza tonight" or "I have a taste for pizza." Or it could be that you have both been thinking it's time to take a vacation or get away for the weekend. Maybe both of you felt like taking a walk in the park, or visiting a relative or friend. Thoughts even will come about giving a certain amount of money to your church or another ministry. Invariably, this will happen; you will hear your thoughts or feelings lining up to be the same one day.

You have made your marriage vows, declaring before God that you shall become one—one body that cannot be divided. No longer are you two individuals, but one. With due diligence, stay in the attitude of being whole and complete, not allowing anything or anyone to meddle and upset your unity. The woman is bone of her husband's bones and flesh of his flesh. God specifically stated that man shall leave his father and mother and be joined to his wife. In other words, you leave to cleave, and nothing and no one should be allowed to interfere in this relationship, to disturb or hinder it. This includes your father, mother, siblings, children, or anyone else. Some enter their marriage giving permission to their parents, even children from a previous union, to have a voice in how things should be done. This can be a catastrophe in a marriage, causing division rather than togetherness. Keep other folks out! Their way of doing things may not help your newfound union. As a newlywed couple, a foundation prayer to pray over your marriage is: "God has joined us together, and we will not allow any man to divide us. No one! Not even us!"

Therefore what God has joined together, let not man separate.

Mark 10:9

The Amplified Bible says, ". . . let not man separate or divide." You can go further in your prayer and include that you will not give permission to man to come in and separate or divide your marriage. And remember that "man" includes you yourself. Don't allow *yourself* to get in the way either to separate what God has joined together. Some may say, "Well, God really did not join us together; it was our flesh" as an excuse to be released from marriage, but actually, when you vowed before God, He recognized your union and joined you together to become one. You are newlyweds; focus on enjoying and learning about one another. Get involved at your local assembly, and stay committed. Watch and pray for each other. Be wise and attentive to having a sound marriage without having too many outside voices speaking to you. Listen to and study the Word of God. Work on seeing things eye to eye when it comes to your finances, children, and church, where God will have you both to be. He has put you together for a purpose and has a perfect plan intended for you. Learn that it's okay to disagree without allowing the enemy to blow things up bigger than what they really are. Invite God into your everyday affairs, so that He may lead and guide you. Acknowledge Him in all your ways, and let Him, not others, direct your path. People do not get married with the idea that they are waiting to get a divorce. No, you get married with hopes of staying together for a lifetime. You said, "I do," not, "I don't." Now you have to apply biblical principles to do just that. Marriage will take some work; if it is not fed, it will starve, shrivel, and shrink.

In previous chapters, I have given this advice: Husbands, learn how to love your wives as Christ loved the church and gave Himself for it. Wives, submit yourselves to your husbands. But I must say that there is Scripture that tells us of submitting to one another. You should both keep in mind that there's another person to consider in the household besides yourself.

> Giving thanks always for all things to God the Father in the name of our Lord Jesus Christ, submitting to one another in the fear of God.
> Ephesians 5:20-21

We often hear the quote that wives are to submit to their husbands, which is a true statement from the Word of God given in the twenty-second verse of the given chapter. But we should not leave out the other, of submitting to each other in the fear of God. So what does that mean? I believe it means we are to consider the other person's feelings just as important as our own. When we do this, we are not being selfish. This marriage union is not just about one person only, *you*. When you said, "I do," you implied that you would perform love actions for the other. A wedding ceremony requires witnesses of the spoken confession you made, the words "I do." Some make up their own vows to speak to each other; nevertheless, they, too, were a promise of a love with a guarantee. A marriage union is a lot like when you confess with your mouth to the Lord Jesus to be saved. You come into relationship with the Lord to have and to hold. The only difference is with the Lord, it's not until death do you part, but together for eternity. Let's look at some similarities between the marriage union and your relationship with the Lord. The Lord does not want you to go outside of Him and commit sins against Him. Your relationship with the Lord should always be a **faithful** and **committed** one. Likewise, it should be so in your marriage union. You **communicate** in prayer with the Lord. You also should make sure you are in **communication** with your spouse. **Communication** is essential when in a relationship. If you never truly **communicate**, the relationship experiences somewhat of a separation, and this may open doors for other negative things that will harm the relationship. Always have a line of **communication** going, especially positive **communication**. Learn to speak the answers and not the problems. Don't be so critical of each other. Remember, the Lord loves you, and He does not judge you. **Intimacy** is also a key factor in both your marriage and your relationship with the Lord. Make sure you are finding time to spend with your spouse, keeping the closeness. **Intimacy** is not possible with only one person; it takes two to tango. You are to desire and pursue **intimacy**. It's not a difficult endeavor. Think of your love for the one whom you chose to marry and who this person is in your life; keep the passion alive. You may have to put aside some things if they are hindering your **intimacy**. In both your marriage and your relationship with the Lord, you come to know each other by means of **intimacy**. It gives you a closeness that will bind you together like glue, and without it, you stand a chance of losing security. **Time** is another desire. God wants you to spend quality **time** with Him, in His Word, in prayer, and in His presence. Likewise, set aside **time** for each other in your marriage. Have a date night once a week or whatever best suits your schedules. Manage to have valuable **time** for fun and enjoyment. You married this person to spend **time** with him or her, not to be away from that person. The reason why there are so many divorces is that during the process of becoming one, people quit. They will not handle the demands of blending into a mold of oneness. Someone is being selfish if he or she is not ever willing to make **time** to spend with the other; this is not the will of the Lord. If each individual will look on how he or she can please the other, the marriage will be a much happier and a more joyous one.

There is work required of each of you; you both must do your part in order to build a good Christian marriage. You need to make sure that, as much as possible, you are attending a church together, one that teaches the truth of God's Word. Make sure you are *there* more than you are *not there* together. Don't make excuses for not attending; you will grow and become stronger as one when you are in the presence of God. As well, take time at home to do spiritual things together, such as praying, watching Christian television programs, reading the Bible, or studying the Word together. Talk about the things of God together without trying to change each other. Talk about the goodness of God. See the good in each other, and bring those good things forth, instead of finding fault with each other. When the challenges come, don't give up so easily and throw in the towel too quickly. Instead, fight the good fight of faith. Leave out harsh words when speaking to each other. If they should come, the spouse who receives them should give a soft answer instead of responding with the same harshness. Why?

> A soft answer turns away wrath, but a harsh word stirs up anger. The tongue of the wise uses knowledge rightly, but the mouth of fools pours forth foolishness.
>
> Proverbs 15:1-2

There's a choice to make: Which one would you prefer to have, a soft answer or a harsh word? Choose wisely according to the outcome that you desire. You may feel pretty heated, but be careful how you react with your words. Do not resort to name-calling, beating each other up, only to one day feel so much love again and think, *Why did I do that?* Stay on the side of peace, and never give in to words that will hurt and scar. Do what needs to be done to have an atmosphere of love again. Someone should be humble enough to get peace back, and get rid of anger, before he or she goes to bed. Anger is an emotion from your soul, but you are not to be ruled by your soul, but by the Spirit of the Lord that dwells in you. Don't go to bed angry; get rid of the anger before the sun goes down. Don't give any place to the devil in your marriage or in any situation.

> "Be angry, and do not sin": do not let the sun go down on your wrath, nor give place to the devil.
> Ephesians 4:26-27

I can recall sleeping on the edge of the bed because I did not want to be near my husband, and I didn't want any contact at all, not even in the smallest way. One day the Lord dealt with my heart on this, and I told Him, "Deal with Mike; he's the man, the head. You made him first, so why do I have to be the one to ask for forgiveness or get this issue resolved?" Nevertheless, God had dealt with my heart, and it was I who was to obey. So whomever the Lord is dealing with is the person who is to obey. I will say that to whom much is given, much is required. When you come into knowledge of the Word of God, you are accountable to be a doer of it. You should know that it all works together for your good. Therefore, continue learning the Word of God, that it may be applied in your life for the good of it. You may feel you are always the one apologizing and repenting. It will be okay. Someone has to do it. Continue to do what is right and pleasing in God's sight. Just because you are newlyweds does not exclude you from having tests and trials in your relationship. Love each other, keep strife out of your marriage, and stay committed to God and the marriage union. Enjoy your days of growth together. Marriage is not always an easy ride, but you will never regret beginning this precious journey together built on Jesus Christ, an unshakable foundation. You may feel like quitting and giving up, but don't. You are two hearts that have been joined together. No matter who you are with, every person is unique and a different individual.

Learn to talk things over and confide in each other. Enjoy life, laugh together, and support each other. After all, God never intended for us to be alone.

> And the Lord God said, "It is not good that man should be alone; I will make him a helper comparable to him."
>
> Genesis 2:18

God has kept you from having loneliness in life, and during your wedding ceremony, you most likely said, "I do." Words are powerful, having the ability to give life or death. Now that you are married, practice saying these "I do's" often:

- "I do" love my wife like Christ loved the church and give myself to her.
- "I do" give my life for her.
- "I do" willingly submit myself to my husband.
- "I do" respect my husband.
- "I do" enjoy quality time with my husband/wife.
- "I do" read the Bible and apply it to my life.
- "I do" attend church with my husband/wife.
- "I do" have a heart to have and keep peace in my marriage.
- "I do" take time to pray for my husband/wife.
- "I do" keep God in my marriage and others out.
- "I do" have communication, intimacy, and quality time with my husband/wife.

Take pleasure in your marriage journey, knowing that inevitably, you will find that no one is perfect. You just have to keep the one and only perfect Person, Jesus Christ, in union with you to help establish you in marriage.

The test: Living with a new person.

The trial: A commitment to the marriage union.

The testimony: The husband and wife, enjoy each other in the fear of the Lord, and also having learned how to live and grow together. We are speaking the Word of God and the "I do's," as we become one, watching and praying for each other.

Pray this prayer: *Father, we come to You in Jesus' name to help our newly joined together union, our marriage. Help us to love each other unconditionally; help keep our words soft and away from anger. Should one of us become angry, help us by reminding the other to give a soft answer. We are very much aware that we have made vows before You in matrimony. We ask that You stir our hearts toward being in church together and spending time in Your Word. Teach us Your ways, that we may obey them. Help us, Father, to keep ungodly counsel out of our marriage and to seek godly counsel when we feel we need it. We honor and thank You for allowing us to have a marriage whereby we can bring forth fruit unto You. In Jesus' name we pray. Amen.*

Pay Attention

My son, give attention to my words; incline your ear to my sayings.

Proverbs 4:20

D o you walk around with your eyes wide open and your ears closed? Do you notice everything that you see around you, and not pay attention to the Word of God that you are hearing with your spiritual ears? Pay attention, and listen to the Spirit of the Lord, who speaks to you by His Spirit and His Word. Pay attention to what is being said to you. It's important and will keep you safe from harm's way, whether in your marriage, in your family, in church, on the job, or even in a court of law. Some may think details are unimportant small things to be ignored. I beg to differ; the small, little details can have the potential of becoming something big. Therefore, pay attention to them!

How many doctors, nurses, lawyers, and businessmen will continue to be successful and keep customers satisfied if they are not paying attention to the small details? An athlete or coach pays attention to the small details to calculate a strategy whereby the team may win the game. A fireman has to be quick to pay attention to sudden changes in a fire situation. What he does matters in a life-or-death situation. People who pay attention are generally people who want to learn how to make things better.

Let's look at a marriage situation: Your spouse is speaking to you about an important issue. Bring to a standstill whatever you may be doing, and pay attention to what is being said to you, giving thoughtfulness and consideration. If you are watching television, or reading the newspaper, a magazine, or a book, stop long enough to listen to what is being said, and you can avoid hearing, "Did you hear what I said?" Even in that, don't just appear to hear with a solemn look on your face while tuning your spouse out. Really listen. Give your undivided attention, and sincerely pay attention to every word said. When speaking, no one wants to feel he or she is being ignored, but that the person being spoken to is giving attention to every word spoken. The Scriptures tell us the importance of paying attention to His Word and wisdom:

> My son, give attention to my words; incline your ear to my sayings.
>
> Proverbs 4:20

> My son, pay attention to my wisdom; lend your ear to my understanding.
>
> Proverbs 5:1

One morning at around 3 A.M., I was awakened and heard within my spirit, "This is the day that the Lord has made." I went back to sleep, and awoke again around 5 A.M., hearing the Spirit of the Lord say, "This is the day that the Lord has made." Then when I awoke for the day at around 7 A.M., I heard again, "This is the day that the Lord has made." Knowing this was the third time I had heard this, I came in agreement immediately with that word by completing the sentence and personalizing the conclusion of it. I said, "And I will rejoice and be glad in it." Later that day, my husband and I got into a big disagreement, and I was highly upset, to the point that my head hurt. As I sat quietly, hurting, I heard, "Let it go, Pat," and then, "We will rejoice and be glad in it." I knew that the Holy Spirit had come to comfort me. He knew beforehand that I would have this challenge this day and gave me the first part of this Word mentioned in Psalm 118:24. Then, later in the day, the Spirit of the Lord said, "We will rejoice and be glad in it." God knew I would need His Word to stand on to be sustained; therefore, in advance, He sent His Word to me so that I may line up, speak His Word, and be healed of what was to come challenge me. Psalm 107:20 tells us, "He sent His word and healed them, and delivered them from their destructions." It pays to pay attention to the Word of God, be it written or sent to you by the Spirit of the Lord. The centurion understood that Jesus needed only to speak a word, and his servant would be healed (Matthew 8:8). Deliverance comes to those who pay attention and yield to what has been given.

To "pay" is to give, or render, what is due, to compensate, make and give an equal return. Another way to put it is, if someone is speaking, in return, there should be someone listening. Know that people are inclined to pay attention for a limited time, especially when they are not interested in what's being shelled out to them. When I owned and operated a child-care center, the education I received concerning children was that their attention span is usually no more than one minute for each year of the child's age. In other words, if a child is five years old, you can look to get no more than five minutes of his or her willingness to give attention before the child wants to do something else. With adults, you max out at about twenty minutes in attention duration.

Other studies show that the average attention span is really only eight seconds before distraction sets in. This is true because a person can be looking at something, and it won't be long before the person is distracted and looking elsewhere. Have you ever been praying and had other thoughts come to mind? At work, people focus their attention on a given task in order to satisfy their job description, and within twenty minutes, they may begin to feel distracted. As they look away for a few seconds and gaze out the window, their bodies become somewhat fidgety. They may turn their heads from side to side to relieve tension, get on the telephone, twirl their pen or pencil, talk with a coworker, and get up for a bathroom break.

So many distractions! Why must we work at paying attention? Let me answer that question for you. The human mind is always wandering. The body has many parts, and they all want activity in order to have fulfillment. The ears hear what's going on around them, and the head assists the eyes by turning to see its surroundings. The arms may want to be stretched or reach for something; the hands and fingers want movement, so they pick up or hold things. The thighs, legs, and feet want to get up and move around. You see, the body is not dead; it has living, functioning parts that all have a call of duty. Therefore, it takes a conscious effort to focus and pay attention. To pay attention, all your body parts must somehow be tuned in, all comfortable, but attentive.

Paying attention should be sincerely worked on in marriages. Don't take each other for granted. Instead, do your part, and pay attention to how you may contribute to your husband's or wife's needs in the relationship. If your spouse is telling you he or she needs time with you, then *pay attention*, and do something about it. If your spouse is saying it, he or she is in need of it. Ignoring what is being said to you makes the other person feel unimportant. You may have to make time to meet that need if that is his or her request. Never be too busy, allowing everything else to take priority over your spouse. If your spouse knows you are at least arranging time for him or her, it will give your spouse something to look forward to, and help keep hope alive.

My husband has always been a very busy man, known to work, work, work, and work some more. I once had a habit of calling him a workaholic, and was getting just what I kept calling him, "a workaholic." So I stopped calling him that, and instead, I say, "My husband loves me, like Christ loves the church, and 'gives himself' to me." He knows that time is a factor for me, and he will make an effort to give me time, sometimes even with an occasional weekend getaway. Sometimes we get quiet and watch a sport together that we both enjoy, such as basketball, or we watch a movie together. I love spending quality time with my husband, and I'm thankful when I get it. Some people are struggling to keep their marriages afloat, but their problems can be solved if they will just pay attention to what the other one needs.

If you need to get understanding and learn how your spouse operates, you can always pray for wisdom and read your Bible. You also can invest in good Christian marital books, audios, and Christian videos to learn ways to succeed in your marriage and God's way of doing things. Ask your spouse how you can help fulfill a need; I'm sure he or she will tell you, knowing that you cared enough to ask. Make sure you are ready to pay attention closely once you are told, and don't add problems, but contribute to the enhancement of the marriage.

Let's look at the differences between men and women and what they can, without difficulty, pay attention to, starting with the men, who usually comprehend their ability to work and provide financially for the home. They, too, may pay attention to tending the lawn, repairing the car, keeping oil and gas in the car, and fixing plumbing or other things around the house that need attention. What may be lacking is the husbands' ability to pay attention to "love" in their marriage and pay attention to their wives. The husbands may not realize the importance of spending quality time with their wives and listening to them when they are speaking. Your wife will know when she has your undivided attention, so it will be wise for you, her husband, to pay attention to her. Pay attention to her needs, and put effort into providing them for her. Pay attention to making sure she takes first place over others, including the children. She does not want to feel that she takes second place to anyone outside God in your life. Hopefully, you are not one to degrade her around others; if so, stop it! This is your wife, not a person on display for your amusement or someone of whom you can make a mockery. You'd better pay attention! Whatever a husband does to his wife, he is doing to himself.

Men like to conquer things, and if they have not been achieving this, it can cause a person to wonder why. If things are not going so great financially or in the workplace, take a look at the condition of the love and behavior toward your wife. If a husband has wounded his wife's heart, he is reflected in the marketplace as one wounded. Oh, yes, it will come out somehow or some way. Sooner or later, it will be a reflection of the husband. There is a spiritual law taking place that can be in a husband's favor or not in his favor. Husbands, are you faithful and devoted to your wife? Can your wife depend on your commitment to her? Read what God said about the treachery of infidelity, taken from several verses from the Amplified Bible:

> And this you do with double guilt; you cover the altar of the Lord with tears [shed by your unoffending wives, divorced by you that you might take heathen wives], and with [your own] weeping and crying out because the Lord does not regard your offering any more or accept it with favor at

your hand. Yet you ask, Why does He reject it? Because the Lord was witness [to the covenant made at your marriage] between you and the wife of your youth, against whom you have dealt treacherously and to whom you were faithless. Yet she is your companion and the wife of your covenant [made by your marriage vows]. And did not God make [you and your wife] one [flesh]? Did not One make you and preserve your spirit alive? And why [did God make you two] one? Because He sought a godly offspring [from your union]. Therefore take heed to yourselves, and let no one deal treacherously and be faithless to the wife of his youth. For the Lord, the God of Israel, says: I hate divorce and marital separation and him who covers his garment [his wife] with violence. Therefore keep a watch upon your spirit [that it may be controlled by My Spirit], that you deal not treacherously and faithlessly [with your marriage mate].

Malachi 2:13-16 AMP

God is not pleased with men who have dealt treacherously with their wives, those who have been disloyal, unfaithful, and deceitful. God loves faithfulness, truth, and loyalty. Although divorce happens, it's the separation that God hates, for it has divided what was joined together. God is not into divisions and things that take away. He's a God who adds and multiplies. Thank God for His grace and mercy. We also can see in the New Testament how the Pharisees came to Jesus to test Him on the law concerning a man's divorcing his wife without any real reason. Jesus reminded them of how in the beginning God made them male and female, and for this reason man shall leave his father and mother and be joined to his wife, and the two shall become one flesh. Also what God has joined together, let not man separate. And yet the Pharisees still questioned him:

> They said to Him, "Why then did Moses command to give a certificate of divorce, and to put her away?" He said to them, "Moses, because of the hardness of your hearts, permitted you to divorce your wives, but from the beginning it was not so. And I say to you, whoever divorces his wife, except for sexual immorality, and marries another, commits adultery; and whoever marries her who is divorced commits adultery."
>
> Matthew 19:7-9

Though Moses permitted divorce, Jesus said, "but from the beginning it was not so." Jesus did not come to put an end to it, but He came to fulfill the law. When a man finds a wife, he has found "a good thing, and obtains favor from the Lord" (Proverbs 18:22). Keeping that favor with the Lord is dependent upon how you are treating your wife, as noted in Malachi 2:13-16.

Husbands, are you truthful *with* your wife? I trust that you are not treating her deceitfully or being unfaithful. God forbid if a husband is violent with his wife. Violence, outside of fighting and aggression, also can be found in meanness, spitefulness, unkindness, heartlessness, or even nastiness toward her. Is she always in tears? Why is that? She is made to be loved, and God gave her to the husband to love. If a husband does not love his wife, he is not pleasing God. Pay attention that you are keeping away from anything that may lead to divorce. To have a good marriage, learn how to solve and evolve. Pay attention to the positives and negatives, no matter how small and insignificant they may seem. It's the little things that can make or break you if you allow them to do so. God sees all things and knows all things. There are Christian homes where wives are living with their husbands' behaviors that do not reflect love. Yet they come to church with a wounded wife, who's hurting on the inside because of how she has been treated. Husbands, don't pretend or ignore what is going on. Ignoring her, not being attentive to her heartache, only adds more pain and suffering. Again, I say, "Solve and evolve," and go on to become all that God wants for both of you as one in marriage.

When I got married, I could not understand why people who have been married for a long time wind up getting a divorce. After many tests and trials, along with corrections, I now understand why people who have been married twenty or thirty years or more get divorces. It seems to others like a sudden boom! What? Divorce happens. But it didn't just suddenly happen. In the previous years, things went ignored, and there was a lack of proper love and care in the marriage, or just plain selfishness without consideration of the other person. Someone did not pay attention to what was being said to him or her; little or nothing happened to make any necessary improvement. More than likely, the one who has expressed himself or herself over and over got tired of fighting the good fight of faith in the marriage and concluded, since there was little or no change, he or she wanted out. That's selfishness! Why are people so selfish? If you are that selfish, why did you get married? Once you marry, it's not all about *you*. You have to get *you* and *your* way in order and look to helping the other person.

Most likely, all the signs were there, but someone continued to ignore them. Signs are for a reason. If you do not pay attention to the signs and heed them, there can be a catastrophe. Using traffic signs as an illustration, think of someone who has ignored a warning sign and speeds right through, perhaps causing an accident. Why did this happen? Someone did not pay attention to the signs. Whenever you approach a stop sign, it is not a sign for you to just slow down. The stop sign means for you to do just that, stop. Paying attention to a sign warning you that you are approaching a curve, you will slow down so your vehicle can safely take that curve. If you ignore the warning and are still driving at a higher speed, you could possibly cause yourself, your vehicle, and even other people on the road to be in harm's way. It was not the sign's fault. It did its job and warned you; all you had to do was pay attention, obey the sign, and slow down. It is only when the signs are ignored, given no attention, or disobeyed that you reap the consequences. In the same way, you are to be sensitive to the signs in your marriage. One major sign to look for and pay attention to is "love." Make sure love is in the air; pay attention to your love walk, and don't ignore the signs. Love never fails; it is never selfish or wanting its own way.

> Love suffers long and is kind; love does not envy; love does not parade itself, is not puffed up; does not behave rudely, does not seek its own, is not provoked, thinks no evil; does not rejoice in iniquity, but rejoices in the truth; bears all things, believes all things, hopes all things, endures all things. Love never fails.
>
> 1 Corinthians 13:4-8

You can take this text and apply the "love" signs. It also will help to keep you away from all the warning signs that denote danger, which are unkindness, envy, selfishness, haughtiness, rudeness, angriness, evilness, and wickedness. Love is the sign that is the opposite of these and will carry you further than any problem. Love looks beyond the flaws. Love will carry you over on the side of commitment.

Husbands, if you are not willing to love your wife according to the Word of God, ask yourself, Why did I get married? Stop! Notice the signs of your love walk that you have toward her. If you are not feeling this love, you should pray that it is restored. God is able to make all grace abound. Make the necessary changes on your part, because when your wife's deepest need, love, is lacking, she may give negativity in your surroundings. *Love* is the key that will open the door to success in your marriage. Make sure you are not giving more attention to other things than you are to the most valuable thing, which is your family. Love can be known only from the actions it prompts. You are to have *agape* love toward your wife. *Agape* is a Greek word meaning an unconditional love for her, a deep and constant, never-ending love. WOW! That's love.

> Nevertheless let each one of you in particular so love his own wife as himself, and let the wife see that she respects her husband.
>
> Ephesians 5:33

You are to *love* not someone else, but your *own* wife as yourself. Paul is speaking in the above text of the *agape* love that a husband should have for his wife.

In this chapter, I've spoken so far primarily to husbands. Now, let's look at wives. They are generally good at being aware of and paying attention to things needed in the household, like toiletries, cleaning supplies, and groceries. They are usually the ones who clean the house, do most of the cooking, and notice when the children need new shoes. Women are equipped to nurture and take care of these things, and are good at multi-tasking. But could women possibly be lacking in the area of paying attention to and giving the respect that's due their husbands? He is your covering, and it is important to him to have you respect him. He needs, values, and deserves it from you. He has been placed as the head in the marriage, which is a great responsibility, so esteem him as such.

If you feel you need to say much, make sure you are giving words of appreciation. Give him admiration and agreement instead of showing your disapproval. Let your demeanor be pleasing in the sight of God and also your husband. It's not all about your having your way all the time. Your husband wants to be loved also. Why is it that the text above does not indicate for and command the wife to show *agape* love to her husband? She is already equipped; God created a woman and designed her to do just that. A wife generally does not have a problem with *agape* love, unconditionally loving her husband. The challenge for her and what he needs is the wife's *respect* and endorsement. When Paul was speaking in Titus 2:4 concerning the older women teaching the younger women to love their husbands and their children, he was speaking of a *phileo love*. *Phileo* is a Greek word meaning having "tender affection." It's about feelings, being friendly toward someone. In the daily wear and tear of life as a wife, you may lack the *phileo love* since it's a love based on the fondness of the heart, and depending on what you may be feeling, this *phileo love* may come up short and come across as your not liking someone. Here's an example of *phileo love* I remember telling my husband, "I love you today; tomorrow I might change my mind." With all sincerity, the motive of *agape* love is there with you. Just work on the *phileo* love, should you have mood swings. Wives, you are to respect your husbands, whether they come across as loving or not, and regardless of how you may feel. Everyone has to do his or her part, regardless of what the other one may be doing. Pay attention to the behavior that you are displaying, and if change needs to take place, make the necessary change. God has given the wife the ability to help win him over back to obedience to Him, if the husband is in disobedience to

Him. You, too, are to deliberately show respect to him. If you work outside the home, pray and ask God for His wisdom, for you have to juggle many tasks. You do not want anything to hinder you from being the keeper of the home. Make sure you are not so beleaguered by work duties that you become alienated from your primary place and purpose that was arranged by God. The virtuous woman in the book of Proverbs was very active at work; she managed many things, yet she took care of her household.

> She is not afraid of snow for her household, for all her household is clothed with scarlet.
>
> Proverbs 31:21

> She watches over the ways of her household, and does not eat the bread of idleness.
>
> Proverbs 31:27

I don't believe it is a sin for a wife to work outside the home, but should she do so, she must remember her primary role is to her husband, children, and household.

> That they admonish the young women to love their husbands, to love their children, to be discreet, chaste, homemakers, good, obedient to their own husbands, that the word of God may not be blasphemed.
>
> Titus 2:4-5

Your husband may need your help in the area of finances, and he may have asked you to work. However, do not neglect the teachings concerning your most important responsibility, as a wife and mother. Pay attention that this is your priority. Be watchful, pray, and do not allow disorder in the home, even through the children. You are the wise woman who builds your house to help build an atmosphere pleasing to the Lord.

One day there was chaos in our home, and I remember literally lifting up my hands, praising God so that all in the household could hear—the children, my husband, *and* the devil, who was the author of the chaos. I walked around and thanked God for peace in my home, that my children were peaceful, that they were trained in the way that they should go. I continued to talk to God; they heard and all got very quiet. There was a residue of peace that came down. All were silent, and the glory of the Lord had come down. Praising and worshiping God for who He was in our household got their attention off of the commotion that was going on with them and brought their attention toward God, whereby they were quiet. The entire home's environment changed without my saying one word to them. I just walked, talked, and praised God, and the enemy scattered in the midst of the praise and worship unto Him. As wives, we ought to set the example of a godly household, even in the midst of any turmoil, and not give place to the devil. Stay in constant intimacy with God, and do not allow your emotions to get the best of you and your family. Follow the Lord, and keep peace in the home. I have heard my husband tell someone that his home was a peaceful home that brought joy to his heart. Peace is what I long to walk in and have, and I trust that you desire it as well. Women are known to deal with emotions, but should submit their feelings to God and seek peace. Pay close attention to your moods; you know when they are there. Don't allow them to control you; rather, control them. I remember telling my daughter when she was a teenager to work on controlling her emotions, and that if she did not control her emotions, they were going to control her. Praise God, she has truly come to a place where she has gained better control over her emotions.

You may have to find an outlet for your emotions so you won't inflict them on family, such as going to a quiet place in the house, praying, reading a good book, calling a friend, and going for a ride. Get a babysitter, if needed. Watch something funny on television; laughter does good, like a medicine. Ask family members to give you some alone time for a while without disturbing you. Let them know it's important that you have a break. You deserve to have a break to get peace—from it all, if needed. Know that the household will be fine in your absence for a few hours or so.

Husbands and wives, pay attention, and realize that it's the enemy that comes to destroy your family. Don't tolerate it from him. Come in agreement with the Word of God, and let no circumstance or person separate you, including the two of you.

So then, they are no longer two but one flesh. Therefore what God has joined together, let not man separate.

Matthew 19:6

God did not join the two of you together for you to be separated. Of course, you will have tests and trials in your marriage, but be on guard, and give notice to anything that comes to bring disorder. Don't allow the word "divorce" to come out of your mouth to give life to it. Once someone starts speaking this "D" word, divorce, he or she is putting into position works to divide the two of them. Be slow to speak, giving thought before your mouth goes into action. "Death and life are in the power of the tongue, and those who love it will eat its fruit" (Proverbs 18:21). Choose the side of speaking life in your marriage and family. It is family that is above all outside of God; it's the most important thing in life. Don't get tricked and think any different.

I am sure there are others who can bear witness to losing a loved one. I can. During my dad's and mom's last days here on this earth, they showed little or no interest in things they considered important when they were up and moving around in good health. What they found most important and valued most during their last days here on earth was their time with family and friends. It was not all the stuff that goes on and the cares in this world. It all boiled down to *people* being the most important in their lives and being surrounded with their presence, support, and love. They were not concerned with bills or how they were going to get paid; they did not express anger toward anyone. Their attention was focused on going to be on the other side and spending their final days and hours with the people who loved them.

Spend your time enjoying your family. The enemy cannot destroy family without first separating the husband and the wife. Don't permit that to happen! With you and your spouse in agreement to pay attention to your love for each other, you will conquer any obstacles, making your marriage a lasting and successful one.

The test: To be watchful, and pay attention to things that come to separate you and your spouse.

The trial: Being able to continue in love toward each other in spite of life's circumstances.

The testimony: We have love and respect in our marriage.

Pray this prayer: *Father, I thank You for joining us together in matrimony. Help me to do my part as a husband/wife, to pay close attention to the plots and schemes that come to destroy my marriage. As Your child, I come in agreement with Your Word and will not have anything to do with the* *separation of my marriage. I pray for commitment on my part and that I give thought and am slow to speak words that do not edify. Father, with the help of the Holy Spirit, I will make lemonade from the lemons in my life, or turn around for the good anything sour thrown at me. I will not allow the "D" word, divorce, to come from my mouth to give life to it in my marriage. I will speak the Word of God pertaining to my marriage, and watch and pray over my husband/wife and my family. In Jesus' name I pray. Amen.*

Little Foxes

Catch us the foxes, the little foxes that spoil the vines, for our vines have tender grapes.

Song of Solomon 2:15

The Song of Solomon is a book of love written by Solomon that includes main speakers, one, in particular: the Shulamite bride. She gives a description of the perfect love scenery, absolutely saturated with the best of love. Several times in this book, she tells the daughters of Jerusalem not to stir up or awaken love until it pleases. This should encourage women not to settle for less, but only accept the best when it comes to love. This is a wonderful book to read from the wisest man ever, Solomon, on his perspective of love. The Shulamite knew that if they caught the foxes, their love could continue without being spoiled. That's it! Be quick to catch the little foxes before they destroy the beauty of your love. Foxes are generally small creatures that use a pouncing technique to kill their prey and are famous for raiding henhouses and stealing chickens if they live near people. Foxes' hearing is so sharp they can hear a watch ticking forty yards away. Their incredible sense of hearing helps them to locate their prey through thick grass or even in underground burrows. Foxes are little, are members of the dog family, are known, like cats, to stalk, sneak up to steal their prey, and often play with their catch before they kill it. The thought of such a little creature as a fox having the capability to spoil our vines gives warning to watch for the little foxes; catch them before they destroy what you have. Take notice of the little things that come up in life, and do not allow them to devour anything concerning you.

I remember early in my marriage, my husband and I were outside in the yard, and we saw a bug, for which we both had a different name. The bug was a roly-poly, a pill bug, having the ability to roll its body up like a ball, resembling a small pill. We went back and forth on what type it was. We allowed this conversation about a little bug to bring disruption to our marriage. The bug went about its business, and we were disconnected. Imagine that; a little bug came along, and we were at odds.

Often this happens in many people's lives—little things interfere. You should always be alert to the little foxes that come along to spoil your vine. Little foxes have a tendency to sneak up before you realize they are there. They can pounce on you so quickly, captivating you in their trap. Be watchful, and don't give place to them (Ephesians 4:27). Maybe your spouse has not said, "I love you" lately. Are you going to treat him or her any differently? Why not say the words, "I love you" yourself? The words will return to you. Sometimes if you want something said or done, you should say or do it to get the ball rolling. My husband and I have always been good at saying, "I love you." But there was a time when I did not hear those words, so I let him know it, and he politely said, "I haven't heard you say, 'I love you' lately either." Well, I quickly told him I loved him, and he told me the same, and since then, it's constant; both of us say it all the time. He's back to saying it first; he just wanted to hear me express it sometimes before he did. Everyone likes hearing the words "I love you." Have you ever gotten a new hairdo, and it went unnoticed? Before you get upset, ask if he or she likes your hairdo.

Perhaps your teenage children have not cleaned their room after you have told them several times. Instead of losing your peace or getting upset, try something different, such as keeping the door closed. If you really want to get your message across that you mean business, get in agreement with them for a cluttered room, if that's what they want. Scatter more things around, and if they don't like it, let them know to clean it. Let them know that you were in agreement with them, and you gave them a helping hand. I never did like an unmade bed, and it seemed as if my then teenager was not getting it, no matter how many times I would say, "Make your bed." Even when I politely said, "*Please* make your bed," the bed went unmade. Not knowing how to handle this because the child was too old to spank, I prayed and asked God what could be done to help this teenager to develop the habit of making the bed. One day I was impressed that this is our house, this child did not pay bills here, and if the child preferred an unmade bed, I knew how to come into agreement with this child. I lifted the mattress completely off the bed and leaned it against the wall. If the child wanted to sleep on it, it would have to be replaced. I was not going to do it, because I was in agreement regarding the unmade bed. This child never said anything about this act being wrong or mean. Weeks later, I mentioned that I noticed the bed was being made. I was thankful that I could at the moment come into agreement with the child for a made bed. This child then said, "Well, I don't want my mattress off my bed." I smiled and said, "Good, because the next time it's unmade, I will put the mattress in the garage, and you'll have to go get it." If that does not help, I will give the mattress away to someone who will appreciate having it. The problem was solved. There was never again a challenge with an unmade bed, and I never lost my peace. Don't throw rocks at me for doing this. I was not rendering evil for evil because there was no evil in what either of us did. It was an issue of training and regulation in our home. Besides, in reality, many people do not want the results of the behavior they are displaying, but they are too righteous to judge themselves. However, when they see that same behavior in another person, it becomes clear to them that the behavior is wrong. In other words, we judge rightfully when looking at another person's wrong, but sometimes fail to see the wrong when it's within us. Case in point: King David did not see his wrong until Nathan told him a parable of another man in the same wrong:

> Then the Lord sent Nathan to David. And he came to him, and said to him: "There were two men in one city, one rich and the other poor. The rich man had exceedingly many flocks and herds. But the poor man had nothing, except one little ewe lamb which he had bought and nourished; and it grew up together with him and with his children. It ate of his own food and drank from his own cup and lay in his bosom; and it was like a daughter to him. And a traveler came to the rich man, who refused to take from his own flock and from his own herd to prepare one for the wayfaring man who had come to him; but he took the poor man's lamb and prepared it for the man who had come to him." So David's anger was greatly aroused against the man, and he said to Nathan, "As the Lord lives, the man who has done this shall surely die! And he shall restore fourfold for the lamb, because he did this thing and because he had no pity." Then Nathan said to David, "You are the man! Thus says the Lord God of Israel: 'I anointed you king over Israel, and I delivered you from the hand of Saul.'
>
> 2 Samuel 12:1-7

King David had sinned against the Lord when he walked on his roof and saw the beautiful woman, Bathsheba, bathing. He sent for her, and she came. He lay with her, and she conceived his child. David, wanting to cover up what he had done with Bathsheba, sent to Joab, saying, "Send me Uriah the Hittite, her husband." David's purpose was to send Uriah to go down to his house with hopes that Uriah would lay with his wife, Bathsheba, so it would appear that she had conceived her husband's child.

Uriah did not go down to his house and eat, drink, and lie with his wife while Israel and Judah were dwelling in tents, encamped in the open fields. His heart would not let him please himself, as his fellow soldiers would not have the same pleasure. King David let Uriah depart, with him delivering a letter written to his leader, Joab, telling him to "set Uriah in the forefront of the hottest battle, and retreat from him, that he may be struck down and die" (2 Samuel 11:15). And it was so. King David plotted Uriah's death. A murderer will murder, but does not want to be murdered; people want mercy without giving mercy. This illustrates how there are people who will do unto others what they really do not want done to them, but Jesus said:

> Therefore, whatever you want men to do to you, do also to them, for this is the Law and the Prophets.
> Matthew 7:12

Jesus tells us that whatever you would like done to yourself, do to others. The Word of God also tells us to judge ourselves and not to judge others, yet the nature of people is to see others before they see themselves. If you want to help someone see his or her actions, find an illustration of it that does not include his or her being within it. Then the person will observe what is really taking place, because that person is not judging himself or herself, but someone else. People sometimes think it's others who need a change or fixing before they see it is they who need change or fixing. This behavior starts early in children. When I owned and operated a child-care center, there was a four-year-old who literally would fall on the floor to have a tantrum. This outburst went on a lot, whenever he could not have his way. Again, praying and asking the Lord what to do, one day I came to his teacher's classroom during one of his episodes and tried to calm him, but he continued. I got down on the floor and began to mimic his behavior. Being surprised, he stopped, sat up, touched me, and said, "Ms. Pat, it's going to be okay. Stop crying." Rubbing my eyes, I told him it made me sad to see him fall on the floor, crying. He said he would not do that anymore. Continuing to rub my eyes as if I were crying, I asked him, "Do you promise?" He replied, "I promise." We had no more challenges or outbursts with this child. He did not want me to be sad. Praise God! This illustration allowed him to see his behavior along with his not wanting me to cry. There is a way for others to see themselves, and if they are not judging themselves, with the help of the Holy Spirit, a way can be shown.

In every situation of life, opportunities can be presented that may cause you to lose your peace. Others may get you upset with their way of doing things or how they may treat you. There is an enemy against you, and although it may come by way of people, the enemy behind what's attacking you is really not the people.

Finally, my brethren, be strong in the Lord and in the power of His might. Put on the whole armor of God, that you may be able to stand against the wiles of the devil. For we do not wrestle against flesh and blood, but against principalities, against powers, against the rulers of the darkness of this age, against spiritual hosts of wickedness in the heavenly places. Therefore take up the whole armor of God, that you may be able to withstand in the evil day, and having done all, to stand. Stand therefore, having girded your waist with truth, having put on the breastplate of righteousness, and having shod your feet with the preparation of the gospel of peace; above all, taking the shield of faith with which you will be able to quench all the fiery darts of the wicked one.

Ephesians 6:10-16

What's needed is a uniform, and it's called the whole armor of God, for it will intercept even the smallest darts. The darts of the wicked one described in the text are the "little foxes," your real enemy, the devil behind it all, coming in the form of darts. Darts are small in size, pointed at the end, coming with a bit of a rush in the direction in which they're thrown, similar to little foxes. Don't allow the little foxes that may come by means of the behavior of people to disrupt your peace. Know the source of these little foxes, and tackle them by holding up the shield of faith. The shield of faith is a significant part of your uniform. You will need it at all times to protect and block those little foxes aiming to hurt, harm, or destroy you. Don't be alarmed when people are not doing the right thing. The Bible has given us principles on how to deal with the fiery darts. Continue to bring forth the good, and overcome evil instead of rendering evil for evil. There is always a wise way of doing things without giving the devil any place in your life.

Jesus did not play around with the devil when it came to his tactics. Jesus was not always as mild-mannered as some may think. He knew when and how to speak up against the enemy behind something. When Herod wanted to kill Him, Jesus referred to him as a fox, knowing Herod was someone who wanted to pounce on Him. The Pharisees came to warn Jesus to get out and depart because Herod wanted to kill Him. Jesus responded:

> Go, tell that fox, "Behold, I cast out demons and perform cures today and tomorrow, and the third day I shall be perfected." Nevertheless I must journey today, tomorrow, and the day following; for it cannot be that a prophet should perish outside of Jerusalem.
>
> Luke 13:32-33

Jesus knew what that fox was up to. He was not afraid of the death threats against Him, or of Herod's motives. Do you know what the little foxes are up to in your life? If so, don't be afraid of those little foxes, but be aware of what is going on around you. This will give you the upper hand on how to handle things. There are so many little things that come up in life, and people give in to them, causing people to act out in their flesh, losing an opportunity to have a testimony, along with losing the witness to give God the glory. Little things, as insignificant as they seem, can cause an enormous amount of damage. It's only afterward that one thinks about how something so small has pulled apart loved ones once so precious to the person. There are people who have not spoken to their family members because of some minor little thing. Little foxes have destroyed many relationships that should not have been destroyed. It all can be avoided if only one person is willing to lay aside pride and be of such a humble heart that he or she asks for forgiveness. Things are capable of being restored back to the place that they once were if someone is humble. Who's willing to be the one to take back what the little foxes have stolen? Usually, when little foxes come my way to harm any of my relationships, whether with my spiritual or natural family or my friends, I stop and think before I respond to them. I believe in being a doer, and not just a hearer, of the Word. Without fail, after praying and seeking God's wisdom on the matter, I eventually will go to that person, even if I believe I have done no wrong. Why? To get peace restored in the relationship.

Some things we have already been led to do through the Word of God; therefore, we don't have to justify our lack of action by saying, "I am waiting to be led." There are many Christians walking around, going to church, praising God, and holding grudges with a brother or sister in Christ. This should not be. Get rid of the little foxes, the walls that have caused division among you, no matter where they are coming from. Whether they are in your marriage, family, church, friendships, or workplace, free yourself of them, and walk in the fruit of the spirit of the love of God. Lay aside every weight or sin that can so easily ensnare you.

> Therefore we also, since we are surrounded by so great a cloud of witnesses, let us lay aside every weight, and the sin which so easily ensnares us, and let us run with endurance the race that is set before us, looking unto Jesus, the author and finisher of our faith, who for the joy that was set before Him endured the cross, despising the shame, and has sat down at the right hand of the throne of God.
>
> Hebrews 12:1-2

Weights can be burdensome and heavy and will keep you from fully following Christ. When you lay aside the weights, everything is much lighter, and you are burden-free. We always should be on guard against the little foxes in our lives and not give them place to pounce and cause harm. Are you going to allow something so little to jump all over you to show sin and shame? We are much bigger than those little things. Using a personal example of the impact little things can have, the Lord really had to help me in the area of spiders. I had allowed fear in my life due to such a little thing. If there was a spider in the house, I called my husband and begged him to come home from work to get the spider. I called my dad, who at the time lived about five miles away, to come kill a spider. Once late at night, when my husband was working a night shift, I called on a neighbor, who was sick, to come kill a spider for me. This was an emergency situation to me, and I needed help; as a result, I pleaded with her to come over. She asked me if I was serious. She could not believe what she was hearing, but I was as serious as serious can get. Oh, and know she came over and killed the spider as I stood on the furniture. One day while I was driving the car, I threw the car in park and jumped out of it into traffic. A policeman saw and came over and asked me if I was all right. I told him there was a spider in the car. He drove off and left me standing there. Would you believe he did not come to my rescue? I jumped in my husband's lap at a red light because a little spider came down near my side in the car. He asked me to move, to get off him, and I would not. I was trying to climb over him to get out on the other side. The people in the next lane looked on in shock, not knowing what was going on. Once I moved out of our bedroom to sleep because of a spider, and did not go back in there to sleep until a few days after my husband found and showed me the spider, dead. One day when I was at a restaurant with some of my Christian lady friends who see me as a strong Christian, a spider came down on the side of the booth where I was sitting. What do you think happened? I first tried to climb over the table, screaming, "A spider! A spider!" I pushed my body next to the sister sitting near me to get out. A dear gentleman came over from another table to assist us. My Christian lady friends were as shocked as you probably are reading this. These encounters really happened; my husband and all those who have come to my rescue or were with me can verify them. My husband KNOWS this was something very serious, and as my covering, he knew to pray for me in this area. At one time, he wanted me to take up gardening. Due to the spiders, he does not anymore.

God has protected me and others from harm when facing something as small as a spider. I pray anyone who reads this, and personally knows me, doesn't tempt me with this. Someone possibly could be hurt. But I continually will say, "Praise God, I am free!" The spider *was* a little fox in my life, for God has not given me a spirit of fear, but of power and of love, and of a sound mind.

Little things come with power packed behind them, whether for the good or bad. A flip of a small switch in your home turns power on in order to have light. A key in the ignition of a car, once turned, causes a large engine to start so the vehicle can move. A telephone, a remote, a computer, a drill, a saw, medicine, a bomb, and many other things are small in size, but produce powerful outcomes. The Bible gives examples of little things that are powerful enough that they control the big things.

> Indeed, we put *bits* in horses' mouths that they may obey us, and we turn their whole body. Look also at ships: although they are so large and are driven by fierce winds, they are turned by a very small *rudder* wherever the pilot desires. Even so the *tongue* is a little member and boasts great things. See how great a forest a little *fire* kindles!
>
> James 3:3-5

Do you see the impact behind such small things? Be on your guard, be watchful, and do not allow the little foxes to come in and spoil and ruin your life. Chase them away before they cause you any harm. The apostle Paul provided a spiritual lesson from a physical fact when he stated, "A little leaven leavens the whole lump" (Galatians 5:9). Just a small amount of tolerance of sin and wrongdoings can corrupt people, churches, marriages, families, businesses, political affairs, government, and so much more.

Don't put yourself in a compromising situation. When things are not going your way, are you allowing a little fox to come in and make a mountain out of it? Little foxes are known to steal, and will steal your joy and your peace, if you allow it. Jesus said:

> Most assuredly, I say to you, he who believes in Me, the works that I do he will do also; and greater works than these he will do, because I go to My Father.
>
> John 14:12

> And these signs will follow those who believe: In My name they will cast out demons; they will speak with new tongues.
>
> Mark 16:17

Signs follow the believer, and one of those signs is to cast out demons. Yes, you can chase the devil, the little foxes, away. Thank God, we have power over any works of the devil and can put him to flight. You are victorious, more than conquerors through Him who loved you. Regardless of how many things that may rise up against you, the greater One lives within you to put you over in life, for you are equipped to overcome all the works of the enemy.

> You are of God, little children, and have overcome them, because He who is in you is greater than he who is in the world.
>
> 1 John 4:4

He who is in you is greater than any test, trial, or temptation that comes up against you by way of little foxes. God is on your side, so "resist the devil and he will flee from you" (James 4:7). You may feel that no one has ever gone through what you are experiencing. Temptation is common to man, and God makes a way of escape,

> No temptation has overtaken you except such as is common to man; but God is faithful, who will not allow you to be tempted beyond what you are able, but with the temptation will also make the way of escape, that you may be able to bear it.
>
> 1 Corinthians 10:13

Temptations are common and will come to everyone. What will you do when they come into *your* life? There is no sin in the temptation in itself; the little foxes want you to yield to the temptation by sinning. The trial period will examine and determine your worth, followed by a verdict. However, keep the faith, and turn your temptation into an area of spiritual growth whenever it arises. Read the Bible, pray, resist the temptation, and refocus your thoughts. Think on things that are true, noble, just, pure, lovely, and things that are of good report (Philippians 4:8).

The test: The little foxes that come to spoil the vine.

The trial: How you handle the little foxes when they come your way in life.

The testimony: We can resist the devil and all his tactics, and overcome evil. We have the greater One within us, and can be victorious!

Pray this prayer: *Thank You, Father, in advance for always causing me to be triumphant and victorious. I ask You for Your wisdom on how to deal with the little foxes that come my way. Help me so that I will not give them place to spoil or ruin anything concerning any of my relationships and walks of life. I will not be afraid of what may come at me, for You have not given me a spirit of fear, but of power, love, and a sound mind. I will walk in assurance that You will never leave or forsake me, that You are on my side. I can do all things through Christ who strengthens me. I, with the help of the Holy Spirit, will be attentive and yield myself to Your way of doing things. Father, You are good all the time, and I will endeavor to do good and walk in Your love toward others, that You may be glorified. Continue to keep me from all the works of the enemy, and help me to do my part standing on Your Word. I will put on the whole armor of God and take up my shield of faith to quench all the fiery darts of the enemy. In Jesus' name I pray. Amen.*

TESTS, TRIALS, AND TESTIMONIES

Inside Truths That Will Set You Free
and Change Your Life

PART 2

PART 2

Overcome and Live Victoriously

Everyone, married or not, can benefit from these chapters

The Body

For as the body is one and has many members,
but all the members of that one body, being many,
are one body, so also is Christ.

1 Corinthians 12:12

More than likely, if someone accidentally hit his
or her toe against something hard while moving
around, especially at night, the response would be to
reach down and take hold of the toe. This might be followed by a scream or moan, as well as hopping around
in pain. While it is just a toe, a small part of the body,
it is very much a part of the body, no matter its size
or significance. When the toe felt pain, other parts of
the body reacted. In all probability, the eyes stretched
wide open or closed tightly, the mouth opened to make
a loud sound or closed while groaning, and the arms
went downward to escort the hands in grabbing the
toes. The back may even have bent a little, the knee
and leg helping to push the toe upward to meet the
hand coming toward it. All of the body members worked
together simultaneously for one common goal: to bring
comfort to the toe. The amazing unity they all possessed
is a perfect example of the oneness of the body. Your
body parts are part of the natural man, and God's creation automatically knew to come together in unity no
matter the circumstance. There was not a member of

the body that went away from the toe that was hurting; instead, all joined in with the toe because the toe needed comforting. Now, in an animation, you may see a character whose body parts are disconnected, with the eyes coming out of its head, or the head, arms, and legs popping off, separating during a time of shock. Possibly a train or something horrific was approaching it. That is not reality; it is not flesh and bones as we are. Animation is not the manner God created for us. He has prepared a body that is fitly joined together, with all the members working together for the good, assisting and supporting one another. Unless there has been an amputation or surgery, all parts of the body will stay together, never leaving you. By no means were they intended for separation, but to be in one accord. WOW! God is GOOD! He has given us a perfect example of His creation that can visibly be seen in all or any fleshly creations. Take a good look at the body and how all of its parts work together. When I think of the goodness of God, my soul cries out, *Hallelujah!* I praise God for His mighty works, along with His wonders. God has a function; the body's purpose is to be in unity, in harmony, and in agreement—that beautiful oneness.

The human body with its purpose of unity is the exact design for the function of the spiritual body of Christ. God wants unity, not division, within His spiritual body, born-again believers, Christians. As the natural body has many members to function properly, so does the spiritual body. We were all (not some) baptized into one body with many members, and God has set the members, each one of them, in the body just as He pleased.

But now indeed there are many members, yet one body. And the eye cannot say to the hand, "I have no need of you"; nor again the head to the feet, "I have no need of you." No, much rather, those members of the body which seem to be weaker are necessary. And those members of the body which we think to be less honorable, on these we bestow greater honor; and our unpresentable parts have greater modesty, but our presentable parts have no need. But God composed the body, having given greater honor to that part which lacks it, that there should be no schism in the body, but that the members should have the same care for one another. And if one member suffers, all the members suffer with it; or if one member is honored, all the members rejoice with it.

1 Corinthians 12:20-26

There is one body, yet it has many members. All are necessary, including the weaker ones. Those members of the body that we think are less honorable are bestowed greater honor. People complain because they don't like the shape of their nose, but the nose is an entrance that gives you oxygen, the gas of life! Your nose is helping you live; without it for just a few seconds, what you are visibly looking at will disappear from your view. You can black out and even die from a lack of oxygen coming to you through the doorway of your nose. You may not like the way your ears look, but without them, how would you hear? Ah! The nose, the ears, the less honorable parts you may not admire are the very ones of most significance. Likewise, it is so within the spiritual body parts, the least honorable being someone who does not look good enough or have what you have. You may consider that person to be someone you would not want in your company. People are sometimes not sensitive to the fact that they are allowing schism within the body. First Corinthians 12:25 tells us, "There should be no schism in the body." Why? Schism separates, but God wants wholeness, oneness, unity within the body, not division.

Division does the animation of separating one from another, causing the body not to be in harmony. This is not God's plan! The body is not made to have parts separating and going in different directions. I thank God that I am under a leadership wise at keeping unity within the local body of believers. Love keeps us in unity, and anything that arises to disrupt unity, or divide, should be dealt with. God has put together the body to be in harmony and not to be split apart. A body that has scattered parts will be limited from functioning properly. Make sure you are connected to a local assembly of believers; you cannot survive on your own, without the other members of the body. Years ago when I left my former church, I stayed home, not attending church services (outside of a few occasional visits elsewhere). My church time was in front of Christian television. I allowed myself to be tricked, thinking I was really sick of the ain'ts—oops! I mean the saints. With Jesus and the Holy Spirit as my Helper, there was no doubt that I could make it without them. I was determining to stay saved and not be a part of or affiliated any longer as a member of any church. That lasted about eight months, and then suddenly, my heart started longing for fellowship with the body. I could not do it any longer. I was not going out to the world for fulfillment, and the separation from fellowship and from being in the company of people of the same faith caused me to feel lonesome.

As a result, after visiting a few churches, the Lord settled me in a place where He wanted me to be to increase in maturity in the Lord. You see, I really believed I could have made it on my own, without the saints, but I could not, and neither can you. A missing body part cannot function and be effective alone. Therefore, we are to consider one another to stir up love, and also to collectively assemble ourselves so much the more during these times.

And let us consider one another in order to stir up love and good works, not forsaking the assembling of ourselves together, as is the manner of some, but exhorting one another, and so much the more as you see the Day approaching.

Hebrews 10:24-25

God's design for the body is attachment, not detachment. A "body" part missing in connection with its spiritual family may be like a dysfunctional family member. Displaying common symptoms of behavior more often than not was born from what they have experienced within the family—such as a lack of empathy or compassion, a feeling that no one seems to understand you or have sensitivity toward you, conflicts, unequal or unfair treatment, adultery or sexual sins, divorce, hurt, shame, fear, and disownment. These things do not stir up love and good works, but will only cause the body to be unhealthy in relationship with the others. A healthy body is a strong body working together for the good of its members. When we come together in fellowship, it helps the body to stay in a flowing function because all members are fitly joined together. When God created man, He first formed his flesh and bones. But He did not leave man just flesh and bones. No, flesh and bones only would have caused man to be basically another substance. Man was not complete until God breathed into his nostrils the breath of life, and it was only then that man became active and living.

And the Lord God formed man of the dust of the ground, and breathed into his nostrils the breath of life; and man became a living being.

Genesis 2:7

God knew exactly what He was doing the day He created man in His likeness and breathed into his nostrils the breath of life. God has created a union of body and spirit that joined together may do a work in His kingdom. God is matchless; He is omniscient, having infinite knowledge. Therefore, causing a deep sleep to fall on Adam, He created the woman by taking one of man's ribs. He did not go outside the body and take more from the dust of the ground to create the woman. No! He stayed right inside Adam's body to bring repro-duction of it. Do you think God knew what He was doing? Do you believe there is a message surrounded by God's action of staying within the body that is "one"? Well, yes, of course, there is a foundation and reason for everything God does. God sees the end results, the domino effect, of duplicating everything good that He is. He sees much further than what we can see, and knows His plans for you.

God has a great purpose for the body. The body is not perfect being alone. It needs help. God blew into man's nostrils the breath of life in order for man to become a living being. There is something about the breath of God breathed on man. In the beginning, God breathed into man's nostrils, giving him life so the body could live and function; without the spirit within, the body is dead. The body and the spirit need each other. Without the spirit, the body cannot function. Without a body, the spirit does not have a vessel to dwell in to carry out God's work here on earth. They both work together for the plans and purposes of the Almighty God.

After Jesus was resurrected from the dead, at His first appearance to the disciples, He did something prior to sending them out for the Great Commission. He "breathed" on them. Like His Father breathed on the body of Adam in the beginning to give him life, Jesus breathed on man the breath of life, so they could receive the Holy Spirit. That was twice that the body had to be breathed on, and even to this day, as believers, we receive power when the Holy Spirit comes "upon" us

(Acts 1:8). The Holy Spirit has power over all the works of the flesh, and will keep the body in obedience as you yield to the Spirit. The flesh has desires. (Read more on the flesh in the next chapter.) However, Paul stated that walking in the Spirit will supersede walking in the flesh.

> I say then: Walk in the Spirit, and you shall not fulfill the lust of the flesh. For the flesh lusts against the Spirit, and the Spirit against the flesh; and these are contrary to one another, so that you do not do the things that you wish.
>
> Galatians 5:16-17

Without the help of the Holy Spirit, the body will go its own way to indulge itself. The world offers many things that the body needs, such as foods, body cleansers, exercise, and entertainment. But some people are more concerned with their natural bodies, with things such as being in shape or changing their looks through plastic surgery and face-lifts. Keeping your body in good health does help with length of life, and it should be taken care of. Besides, the body is the temple in which the Holy Spirit dwells; you are not your own to do whatever your body wants to do.

> Or do you not know that your body is the temple of the Holy Spirit who is in you, whom you have from God, and you are not your own? For you were bought at a price; therefore glorify God in your body and in your spirit, which are God's.
>
> 1 Corinthians 6:19-20

The Holy Spirit is with you wherever you go and knows whatever you do. His purpose is to build you up in the body of Christ, lead, teach, comfort and guide you in all truth. Again, you are not your own to do whatever your flesh pleases. The above text says to glorify God in your body and in your spirit. The whole body and spirit should adore and worship God. As you take good care of the natural body, giving it what it needs in the way of good nourishment and exercise, consider a good look inside and examine your spiritual body, remembering you are one of many members of the body. Do you love the brethren? The brethren are members of the body. The Word of God says, How can we love God, whom we have not seen, and hate the brethren?

> But he who hates his brother is in darkness and walks in darkness, and does not know where he is going, because the darkness has blinded his eyes.
>
> 1 John 2:11

> Whoever hates his brother is a murderer, and you know that no murderer has eternal life abiding in him.
>
> 1 John 3:15

> If someone says, "I love God," and hates his brother, he is a liar; for he who does not love his brother whom he has seen, how can he love God whom he has not seen?
>
> 1 John 4:20

If you hate your brother in Christ, you are echoing that you do not really love God. Your brother is part of the body, and the body is Christ's body, and "He is the head of the body, the church" (Colossians 1:18). You cannot hate one without hating the other. Regardless of what our brother has done to us, we are not to hate him; instead, we are to love him. I am not saying we are to love his sin, what he may have done, or what he is doing currently, but we are to love him for what he is, a member of the body. He is obviously blinded if he is not walking upright, so we should not think we are any better just because we are not in his shoes. We are in God's grace. We are not any better; we, too, have sins and shortcomings. And if you show love and patience to your brother, he has a real chance of becoming rehabilitated, for it is the goodness of God that leads man unto repentance. Love never fails; love conquers all things. So, as the Bible tells us, "Put on love."

> Bearing with one another, and forgiving one another, if anyone has a complaint against another; even as Christ forgave you, so you also must do. But above all these things put on love, which is the bond of perfection. And let the peace of God rule in your hearts, to which also you were called in one body; and be thankful. Let the word of Christ dwell in you richly in all wisdom, teaching and admonishing one another in psalms and hymns and spiritual songs, singing with grace in your hearts to the Lord. And whatever you do in word or deed, do all in the name of the Lord Jesus, giving thanks to God the Father through Him.
>
> Colossians 3:13-17

It may not feel or even seem fair to you, but it's right to do this in the body of Christ. Make sure you are doing your part in demonstrating love. Stay occupied until He comes; find the place where you belong so you are working within the body of Christ. Do not disconnect yourself from your local assembly. If you are missing in action, the body has a void and cannot be whole and complete. Be faithful to the body, doing good service, whereby the member that you are will be helping the body to stay whole. You are a part of the body; you are one with the body, and you are of most significance. The body needs you! So stay connected.

The test: Functioning within the body, not outside the body.

The trial: Staying connected and faithful to the body of Christ.

The testimony: Having become one with the body, connecting and flowing in one accord, the body receives the help it needs to succeed in what God has in store for it.

Pray this prayer: *Father, I thank You for joining me to the body of Christ. I recognize that every member of the body is a family member. I will love the body as I love myself, for we are all one in You. Holy Spirit, remind me of God's Word, that I am not my own, but I am bought with a price. Whenever my body wants to take steps toward a wrongdoing, something not pleasing to You, I ask You to prick my heart. You are my Lord, my Helper. I will examine the body more cautiously, knowing that what I do to it, I am directly doing to myself. Forgive me, Father, of any sins that I have committed against the body, Your body. I will exercise love toward the brethren, no matter how things look or how I may feel, so that You may be glorified, Father. In Jesus' name I pray. Amen.*

The Flesh Is a Mess

There is therefore now no condemnation to
those who are in Christ Jesus, who do not walk
according to the flesh, but according to the Spirit.

Romans 8:1

When you look at what the flesh is actually made
of, you can understand why it is always in need
of a cleaning. God formed and shaped Adam out of the
dust of the ground. Dust is something we believe should
be cleaned up inside the house. Although we dust inside
our houses, the dust always seems to come back. If
you are outside while the wind is blowing dust from
the earth, you will probably cover yourself up to mini-
mize your exposure to it. Dust blows all over, landing in
neighborhoods, on cars, and in homes, and generally
people are not interested in having it around. Dust is
the material flesh was made out of; therefore, I say the
flesh is a mess. The flesh made from dust should not be
followed after, because like the dust, it's usually messy
and not wanted. The word "mess" is defined as a dirty or
untidy condition. It can even get a bit disorderly and is
always in need of being cleaned. If we do not bathe, the
flesh will build up more particles of dust, or dirt, and
perhaps start becoming a little smelly.

Most people are not about living day after day without
putting something on to camouflage their flesh. Soaps,

deodorants, colognes, and other body fragrances are used to cover up the natural smell of the flesh. I like to call it putting "foo-foo" on it, meaning *fooling* the flesh. Along with scenting the skin, we clothe the flesh to cover it from exposure, which should be done. Because the flesh has all these cover-ups, it is a good reason why we should not look at the outward appearance of a person. One day the Holy Spirit said to me while I was sitting in church, "Look around." I turned my head to the right side and looked. I heard again, "Look around." In obedience, I turned my head to the left side and looked around. Once again, I heard, "Look around." Knowing that I was to see all around me, I literally turned my body to look all around me. Right after I looked and then turned to face forward again while sitting, I heard the Spirit of the Lord say to me, "Everything (everyone) is not as it appears to be." At the time, this ministered to me because I was having thoughts that everyone else was much more spiritual, and looked the part. The Holy Spirit was showing me that God looks at the hidden person, which is the heart, and not the person's outer appearance.

Truth and knowledge had come to me of the realization of the true person residing on the inside of us, not visible to others, who are looking on the outside, the flesh. This revelation of God's Word on how man looks on the outside, and how God looks at the heart, caused me to research His Word on it. The Bible says Saul had turned from following God by being disobedient to His commandments; therefore, God rejected Saul from reigning over Israel. God sent the prophet Samuel to anoint another king out of Bethlehem from the sons of Jesse, all whom he invited to a sacrifice to the Lord. After seeing the son, Eliab's physical appearance, Samuel presumed that he had to be the one to anoint, so Samuel spoke, "Surely the Lord's anointed [Eliab] is before Him!" (1 Samuel 16:6).

But the Lord said to Samuel, "Do not look at his appearance or at his physical stature, because I have refused him. For the Lord does not see as man sees; for man looks at the outward appearance, but the Lord looks at the heart."

1 Samuel 16:7

Samuel took one look at Eliab's appearance (his outer shell) and thought he was the one. God sees the heart; he knows the exterior is only a facade, which does not display the real person on the inside. Paul tells us that we are not to put our confidence in the flesh. Let's look at what he said about the flesh:

For we [Christians] are the true circumcision, who worship God in spirit and by the Spirit of God and exult and glory and pride ourselves in Jesus Christ, and put no confidence or dependence [on what we are] in the flesh and on outward privileges and physical advantages and external appearances.

Philippians 3:3 AMP

We are not to put confidence or dependence on ourselves in the flesh, nor on outward privileges, physical advantages, or external appearances. You will merely set yourself up for disappointment if you do put confidence in or dependence on the flesh because the flesh and all that glitters cannot be saved. The flesh disguises itself with a pretense to all who look on it, and to walk according to it will lead to corruption and dishonesty in addition to evil works. Walking in the Spirit will keep one from being tripped up with walking in the deeds of the flesh and lust. The Spirit and the flesh are contrary to each other, as stated in Galatians 5:17: "It is the Spirit who gives life; the flesh profits nothing (John 6:63)." Let's look at what Paul told the Galatians about the characteristics of the various unmistakable works of the flesh:

> Now the works of the flesh are evident, which are: adultery, fornication, uncleanness, lewdness, idolatry, sorcery, hatred, contentions, jealousies, outbursts of wrath, selfish ambitions, dissensions, heresies, envy, murders, drunkenness, revelries, and the like; of which I tell you beforehand, just as I also told you in time past, that those who practice such things will not inherit the kingdom of God.
>
> Galatians 5:19-21

Each of these characteristics is contrary to who and what God is. God is a Spirit, and there is no sin in Him. He is not flesh and blood, seen by the human eye. The "works of the flesh" listed above are not of Him, but are sinful deeds that eventually will come to test you. The flesh has cravings and wants fulfillment, and simply will lead one on the road to much regret and even to destruction unto death. It will be wise to run from such desires and cling to the Spirit that gives life. An example of the repercussions of the works of the flesh is an illegitimate child. You now have a child that may be brought up in a single-home environment without both parents. Later in life, the child's mother becomes a Christian, gets married, and wants to raise the child in a Christian environment, while the child's father still lives a life according to the works of the flesh. Seeing his or her parents living two different lifestyles can cause conflicts and be confusing to the child. There even may be bickering and a power struggle between the two parents. This was not and is not God's best plan for the parents or for the child, but only the after effects that result from previously following the flesh. Family members may voice their opinions to the now married couple in such a position, making such a statement as the child was here before the husband came into the picture. It is as if the child takes priority over the husband (not the biological parent) in the marriage to the child's mother. One must put things in the right perspective and look at the situation from the Scripture, which states: "What God has joined together, let not man separate" (Mark 10:9). I believe this includes even children. I say this because children from either side of the spectrum can grow up and try to cause division between the biological parent and the stepparent. Sadly, some parents have allowed the children to come between them, causing problems and division within the marriage, and even divorce.

Once the mother is married, her husband takes priority, without neglecting the child's needs, as well as supersedes opinionated family members who see the husband as secondary. Outside the wife's relationship with God, the husband and her marriage become the first priority; he is her head. Say later in the marriage, the wife has a child with her husband, only to still hear family members making comments that the illegitimate child takes priority over the child born in the marriage. Picture a child having priority over everyone in the home besides his or her mother. How absurd! This happens due to the lack of knowledge of God's Word. Now, no child should be without a good, healthy relationship with his or her parents. I do believe God wants that relationship and it's His best for all. It's just sad that all the disorder built up that came from outside the marriage (to interfere with the marriage) came from the consequence breathed on from the beginning of walking after the lust of the flesh. Knowing that both children are the mother's, let's look at what God had to say concerning a similar matter with Abraham and Sarah. This instance was produced from a fleshly desire of Sarai, who initially persuaded Abram to go in to her maid, the

Egyptian (Genesis 16:2-5). Later, when facing its aftermath, she wanted to undo it by getting rid of it.

> And Sarah saw the son of Hagar the Egyptian, whom she had borne to Abraham, scoffing. Therefore she said to Abraham, "Cast out this bondwoman and her son; for the son of this bondwoman shall not be heir with my son, namely with Isaac." And the matter was very displeasing in Abraham's sight because of his son. But God said to Abraham, "Do not let it be displeasing in your sight because of the lad or because of your bondwoman. Whatever Sarah has said to you, listen to her voice; for in Isaac your seed shall be called. Yet I will also make a nation of the son of the bondwoman, because he is your seed."
>
> Genesis 21:9-13

Husbands, this text shows it is okay to listen to the voice of your wife, especially if what she is saying is truth and not directing you toward disobedience to God. In the text is a wife who is now displeased with the actions of the bondwoman, the mother of Abraham's firstborn. Sarah's child was the child of promise; the bondwoman's child was born out of works of the flesh. As we look at the New Testament, Paul clarifies that it was according to the flesh and also tells of it being symbolic to us today.

> But he who was of the bondwoman was born according to the flesh, and he of the freewoman through promise, which things are symbolic. For these are the two covenants: the one from Mount Sinai which gives birth to bondage, which is Hagar—for this Hagar is Mount Sinai in Arabia, and corresponds to Jerusalem which now is, and is in bondage with her children—but the

Jerusalem above is free, which is the mother of us all.

Galatians 4:23-26

Now we, brethren, as Isaac was, are children of promise. But, as he who was born according to the flesh then persecuted him who was born according to the Spirit, even so it is now. Nevertheless what does the Scripture say? "Cast out the bondwoman and her son, for the son of the bondwoman shall not be heir with the son of the freewoman." So then, brethren, we are not children of the bondwoman but of the free.

Galatians 4:28-31

These Scriptures demonstrate how what was worked according to the flesh brought persecution to them born according to the Spirit. Things born according to the flesh by anyone can be continual trials that affect the person directly for a lifetime. What was done centuries ago, birthing Ishmael in the flesh, affected what we see in Jerusalem today. Likewise, many people have given birth to things according to the deeds of their flesh, without understanding that the chaos they may be experiencing today is the consequence of their flesh actions. Although God forgives, and His grace is sufficient, His covenant will be established within the right way of doing things. In the case of Abram and Sarai, God had come to get things straight, to clarify His covenant between Himself and Abram. First, God changed their names. Abram, meaning "high father," was changed to Abraham, "father of many nations." Sarai, meaning "dominative and controlling" (look at the meaning of her name alone—the mess that got them into), was changed to Sarah, meaning "princess." All this took place, and still Abraham, having the heart of a father to provide, wanted favor with his son Ishmael, who was born from the flesh to live before God. Although God blessed Ishmael, the son of the flesh, God's covenant was established with the son born from the union of husband and wife. You can read this in Genesis 17:5-21.

All it takes is one flesh act to have a lasting effect on the lives of people. People should take it into consideration before they give in to the deeds of the flesh. Following the flesh will make a mess of things. Therefore, don't follow it. I really want people to see that the flesh is a mess, not in the sense of its having no use, for we need the muscles, the organs, and its interior to help our bodies to function. The flesh is the soft substance of the body that covers the bones and is also covered by layers of skin. It indeed has a need to be covered up, but is made visible by its deeds that are manifested. No matter how you may cover it up, it will be noticeable at times. Allowing the flesh to be in control and following its deeds can affect you, along with many generations. It is sad that children are put in this position as a consequence of sin that they had no part in. As a parent, it's always good to let your child know you are not perfect, that you have made mistakes, yet minister to the child about God's way of doing things and tell the child how everyone has a choice to obey in order to have His best. A person cannot walk after the deeds of the flesh alone without facing the consequences of its works. God is a righteous God and indeed will see that your child is cared for, as He did with Hagar. In Genesis 21:13, God states that He will make a nation out of the son of the bondwoman just because he was Abraham's seed. (I used the example of Abraham and Sarah to articulate to never try to misplace what is right, to justify something that was born from the flesh.) Right is right, wrong is wrong, and there is no way around it. God is a loving and forgiving God; He does not hold things against you. Once you have repented, He doesn't remember your sins any longer. It's a biblical fact that we reap what we have sown. Many people are living in regretful situations after walking after the deeds of the flesh. You may not be able to undo what has been done according to the flesh, but you certainly can get things right with God and allow His wisdom to direct you. Don't get caught up with family or anyone's opinion to the point that you are being fed and led wrongly (more flesh acts) by them. What you may hear from them may sound good with a bit of wisdom to it, but remember that there are two kinds of wisdom. There is a wisdom that is demonic (devilish), and there is a godly wisdom from above.

> But if you have bitter envy and self-seeking in your hearts, do not boast and lie against the truth. This wisdom does not descend from above, but is earthly, sensual, demonic. For where envy and self-seeking exist, confusion and every evil thing are there. But the wisdom that is from above is first pure, then peaceable, gentle, willing to yield, full of mercy and good fruits, without partiality and without hypocrisy.
>
> James 3:14-17

Be watchful of bitter envy and self-seeking in your heart, and do not boast against the truth by allowing anyone or anything to separate you from standing on the side of righteousness.

When my daughter was around age fourteen, she wanted to go on a date with a boy she had been talking with on the phone. She asked if she could go out with him. Both my husband and I would tell her she was not allowed to date just yet. Every time I spoke with her about our concerns, she would say to me that I did not trust her. I responded, "It's not that I don't trust you; I don't trust your flesh." You see, her heart, the real person, believed that she would do right, and there's a possibility she would have. As parents, we were not ready for this and thought it was best that she wait until she is more mature. We have seen many young people get themselves into trouble dating at such a young age. What happens during a date—hand-holding, hugging, kissing, and touching each other—stirs up the flesh and perhaps leads to an act of fornication. Almost of a certainty, it leads to sexual sins, resulting in things within the body like pregnancy, diseases, or sinning against the body. Talking with my daughter, I told her whenever the flesh is touching other flesh, it can lead to something she may regret later. I told her to observe the many young girls who have become pregnant due to their flesh acts, and see if the dads are still around. God's best is not for children to grow up without a father in their lives. It has happened a lot because of temporarily satisfying one's flesh. My daughter, now a young adult, tells me she is so thankful for my talking with her and not allowing her to do some things too early. She was not ready and may have made major mistakes.

Let's put things in the right perspective: We all have flesh, and the flesh occasionally will be tempted. No one should believe temptations come from God. He does not tempt anyone. Temptation comes from the flesh's lustful desires.

> Let no one say when he is tempted. "I am tempted by God"; for God cannot be tempted by evil, nor does He Himself tempt anyone. But each one is tempted when he is drawn away by his own desires and enticed.
>
> James 1:13-14

Some translations read: "But every man is tempted, when he is drawn away of his own lust, and enticed." For what is your flesh lusting/hungering? Are you going to let yourself be attracted to it, persuaded to fall in its trap? Giving your flesh pleasures is not worth having to deal with the consequences afterward. Therefore, put your flesh under submission to the Holy Spirit, and don't yield to its lust. Before you act out what you are about to do in the flesh, think about the effect it will have in the days, months, or years afterward. You do not owe your flesh anything; you are not a debtor to your flesh, but are to surrender to being led by the Spirit of God, for it is the Spirit that gives life.

> Therefore, brethren, we are debtors—not to the flesh, to live according to the flesh. For if you live according to the flesh you will die; but if by the Spirit you put to death the deeds of the body, you will live. For as many as are led by the Spirit of God, these are sons of God.
>
> Romans 8:12-14

Again, "If you live according to the flesh you will die spiritually; but if by the Spirit you put to death the deeds of the body, you will live." My, my, my! All you have to do is exchange following the deeds which the flesh yearns for, to living victoriously according to the Spirit. So if we understand this rightly, we are debtors, all right, only it is to the Spirit and not our flesh that we are duty-bound. We have an obligation to be Spirit-led and live, rather than being led by the flesh and dying. Through daily living, we must be conscious of our walking in the Spirit and that we are not ruled by the flesh. I love the fact that Jesus Himself came in the likeness of sinful flesh and He, too, was tempted in all points, yet He was without sin. He can sympathize with our weaknesses. His example shows us that we are well able to overcome any and all temptations. Yes, Jesus overcame the world, the flesh, and the devil. There is no temptation given to man that he is not able to escape, "because He who is in you, is greater than he who is in the world" (1 John 4:4). The flesh will want things of itself to be satisfied, such as food, water, sleep, cleaning, exercise, and entertainment, all of which are necessary to sustain existence. It's the sinful deeds, contrary to God's way of living, that we are not to provide for the flesh. Do you want good things to happen in your life? If your answer is yes, follow after righteousness. Remember, following after the flesh will make a mess and lead you to have regrets. So search deep within your heart before you make a move and yield yourself to the flesh; really think before you act. If disciplining the flesh becomes challenging for you, and you have no willpower to change from yielding to the flesh, pray and ask the Lord for help. Prayer really does change things. Your flesh may tire you, keep you from even praying, but you have a regenerated spirit to supersede the flesh and press in and pray in spite of how your flesh may feel. At the place called Gethsemane, after He prayed, Jesus found the disciples sleeping and said:

> What? Could you not watch with Me one hour?
> Watch and pray, lest you enter into temptation.
> The spirit indeed is willing, but the flesh is weak.
> Matthew 26:40-41

The disciples were not watching their surroundings, nor were they praying. Had they been doing so, it could have helped them not enter into the temptation soon to come. Jesus knew His time was near to be arrested, and what were the disciples doing? Sleeping! Jesus understood that sleep is a necessity, but the hour was at hand for His betrayal. They should have been alert and ready for what was about to take place. So should *you* be ready for what's about to happen whenever the flesh is at a weakened point.

Often there is a battle going on between the flesh and the spirit. Yielding to the Spirit will always cause you to triumph. Delight yourself toward the inward man, the born-again spirit man, the image of God to serve Him. Choose to follow the leading of the Spirit of God, and be not led by the flesh. Too much flesh pleasure is bound to destroy a person. Do not yield to its lustful desires, as the end results are deadly. Your decisions today will determine your outcome for the future. God's way is the best way. Pursue it!

The test: The temptation of walking after the deeds of the flesh.

The trial: Desires of the flesh with its continual cravings.

The testimony: Yielding to the Spirit of God, allowing the Holy Spirit to lead, and not following the dictates of the flesh. Walking in and having a victorious life in Christ Jesus.

Pray this prayer: *Father, I am always in need of You. I will look to You as my Guide, knowing that my steps are ordered by You. Strengthen me whenever I feel weak. My heart's desire is to follow You in righteous living. Father, I thank You for giving me the Holy Spirit to lead and guide me in all truth. I am not a debtor to the dictates of my flesh. Instead, I will make a conscious decision to live according to the Spirit of the Lord. You are my Source of help. You are my Lord and my Savior. I know You are not the one who tempts me with evil, but it's my own lustful desires. Therefore, I will not surrender myself to my flesh, which would lead me to make a mess. I surrender my will to Your will. I ask You to remind me of the consequences of wrong actions, so that I will immediately get in line with doing things in the way that pleases You. Thank You for life in Christ Jesus, who has made me free from the law of sin and death. I submit all that I am to You. In Jesus' name I pray. Amen.*

Facing the Finger

For God did not send His Son into the world to condemn the world, but that the world through Him might be saved.

John 3:17

I recall an incident in the beginning of my relationship with the Lord, of knowing Him as my heavenly Father and learning how to be led by the Holy Spirit. A sister in the church seemed to dislike me for some reason. Several times when I was in a conversation with another sister in the church, this young lady walked up to us and got in between the sister and me, with her back toward me. She took the sister by the arm or hand and pulled her away from our communication. I had become a little baffled and a bit frustrated as to why she would do this, not once or twice, but many times. It seemed rude to me, and I sensed that she was doing it on purpose.

While sitting in church one Sunday morning, I heard in my spirit, "If your brother offends you, go to him." The Lord even told me that the young woman was in the lobby of the church and to go to her. In obedience to the Holy Spirit, I left the pew where I had been sitting, and sure enough, she was standing at the west end of the lobby. I turned in that direction, but suddenly saw her go into the sanctuary through the west entrance.

WOW! My faith elevated, as I knew this was proof the Spirit of the Lord had spoken to me, for I had no prior knowledge that she was in the church lobby. I wanted to obey the word of the Lord, and I had an opportunity to speak to her that evening at church. Once again, she happened to be in the church lobby. In my heart, I knew not to accuse her, but to point the finger at myself. She was sitting in an area alone, and I sat near her. I said to her, "I wanted to apologize to you if I have done anything that may have offended you." Oh, boy! What was in her surely came out. She did not respond the way I expected. She "ate my lunch," as the saying goes. She quickly placed her finger in my face, very closely, and she let me have it. She told me just how she felt toward me, what she thought of me, and also how I thought that I was "all that"! I was shocked. I did not see this type of response coming at all, especially after being led to go to her. As I sat quietly, listening to her, my feelings were very hurt. She continued with her accusations, along with finger-pointing in my face. This lady expressed very clearly how she perceived me.

I had done nothing to her. All the things she said were her presumptions. Feeling entirely misunderstood and puzzled, yet wanting to have peace between us, I humbled myself, again apologizing for any offense I had unknowingly committed. Leaving her, I was very puzzled. My thought was that since the Holy Spirit had led me to her, everything should have turned out just great. So I asked the Lord if I had missed something: "Lord, this lady and I have had no interaction with each other, no conversations, and no communication whatsoever previously, at least nothing that I can think of that would justify the things she said to me." I had done no wrong, to my knowledge. One day, again, I heard in my spirit, "If your brother offends you, go to him." At that moment, I did not know this was in the Word of

God, the Bible. As a matter of fact, it was afterward that I read what Jesus had said regarding this:

> Moreover if your brother sins against you, go and tell him his fault between you and him alone. If he hears you, you have gained your brother. But if he will not hear, take with you one or two more, that "by the mouth of two or three witnesses every word may be established." And if he refuses to hear them, tell it to the church. But if he refuses even to hear the church, let him be to you like a heathen and a tax collector.
>
> Matthew 18:15-17

As I looked at and read these words that were spoken by Jesus Himself, it sounded like He was telling us to confront and deal with this issue between brethren in the church, not with people of the world. Most people see the word "confrontation" as something negative, but it implies bringing people together, especially for discussion, with the hope of a good outcome. It sounds like what God would want, doesn't it? Sure, an issue could be left alone and ignored, but when it involves a person's heart, the person who has been hurt may well become bitter and resentful. This is not what our heavenly Father would have in the body of Christ. Father God is excellent and knows best how to resolve offense, and He knows that this arrangement will work for the good of both parties involved. What happens in most cases when a brother has sinned against another is the person who has been trespassed against goes to someone else privately, in confidence, instead of going to the person who has done wrong. Possibly the person is thinking he or she is being spiritual by requesting prayer concerning it. This type of action allows someone else's heart to be entangled, and the person may view the offender in a different way than previously. Maybe some are unaware of this instruction given by Jesus, but if you are reading this, you now know this truth.

I just believe that we should do exactly what the Word of God instructs us to do, as an act of obedience; besides, Father knows best. It is the "do" that gets things done. The word *do* is a verb, an action word meaning "to carry out, to perform, to complete, and to act upon." Therefore, we must *do* the word in order to have victory.

> But be doers of the word, and not hearers only, deceiving yourselves. For if anyone is a hearer of the word and not a doer, he is like a man observing his natural face in a mirror.
>
> James 1:22-23

Children need guidance, whether young, middle-aged, or old. We always have the written Word of God and the Holy Spirit to instruct and guide us. We are God's children. We are not fatherless. He will never leave or forsake us. As His children, we are to walk in the light of His Word. Sometimes we are told to do things that our flesh does not want to do; however, it is better to obey than to sacrifice.

Let me get back to the encounter with the lady who just did not like me, and my thinking that I had missed it because of the outcome. When I asked the Lord if I had missed it, I literally heard in my spirit: "You have done your part. Now let me do the rest." I knew to just pray and leave it in God's care. Weeks later at church, while I was standing and talking with someone, the young lady approached. This time she grabbed *me* by the arm, pulling me away. She conversed with me for a long time, as if I were her dearest and best friend. Not once did our last encounter come up. There were no walls, and there was no bitterness, resentment, or hatred in our hearts. Our sisterhood had been healed. Later, the Lord revealed to me that at the time I confronted her, she had too much pride to admit her faults. He had to deal with what was in her heart. He used me to go to her, having her face the issues within her heart. During quiet times, God was able to deal with the real matter in her heart regarding her feelings toward me. She knew in her heart that I had done her no wrong. In reality, we know that the Word of God says Satan is the accuser of the brethren (Revelation 12:10), and he is the real enemy to be put to flight behind this animosity. It was evident that she, too, loved the Lord and wanted to walk in the love of God with her sister in Christ. Therefore, she humbled herself as well to put things in right standing with God. Thank God for the working power of His Word and His children walking in righteousness, which gives victory over offense or wrongdoings.

(For if by the one man's offense death reigned through the one, much more those who receive abundance of grace and of the gift of righteousness will reign in life through the One, Jesus Christ.) Therefore, as through one man's offense judgment came to all men, resulting in condemnation, even so through one Man's righteous act the free gift came to all men, resulting in justification of life. For as by one man's disobedience many were made sinners, so also by one Man's obedience many will be made righteous.

Romans 5:17-19

Like Jesus, when we do what is good and right, we are allowing others to be in right standing with God. Because of Adam's disobedience to God's Word, judgment came. One man, Jesus Christ's obedience to the death on the cross brought many to righteousness. There are times when we have to die to ourselves even when we may know that we are not the one in the wrong in order to win another back into the righteousness of

God. When we follow Christ and obey the Word of the Lord, we can reconcile man unto God. Isn't that what Jesus did? Jesus used Himself as an example, and implemented a word to follow His example.

> Most assuredly, I say to you, unless a grain of wheat falls into the ground and dies, it remains alone; but if it dies, it produces much grain. He who loves his life will lose it, and he who hates his life in this world will keep it for eternal life. If anyone serves Me, let him follow Me; and where I am, there My servant will be also. If anyone serves Me, him My Father will honor.
>
> John 12:24-26

Of course, Jesus is looking at the end results. He died in order to produce not some, but "much" grain. It is interesting that Jesus used a grain of wheat to articulate an example of something or someone dying for the production of much. Did you know that there is a summer and winter wheat? Summer wheat is planted in the spring, and winter wheat is planted in the fall, maturing for the next spring or summer. It sounds like, with grain, you are producing much year round, but the key words are "it dies." Grain in plenty reminds me of the first verse in the American patriotic song "America the Beautiful," which says:

> O beautiful for spacious skies,
> For amber waves of grain,
> For purple mountain majesties
> Above the fruited plain!
> America! America!
> God shed His grace on thee,
> And crown thy good with brotherhood
> From sea to shining sea!

"Waves" of grain and "fruited" plain tell us there was abundance. Now that's production! Jesus wants us to do likewise by following His example, not by dying a real physical death, as He did, but a death of denying yourself so that you may live. Jesus, for a moment, said His soul was troubled. He also stated, "What shall I say? 'Father, save Me from this hour'? But for this purpose I came to this hour" (John 12:27). He knew His purpose and what would be gained; therefore, He denied His life.

The reason I say to go to your brethren is to point you in the direction of triumph, so please do not misunderstand. I am not saying we are to go around finding fault with one another. I am simply saying to obey the Word of the Lord. It just happens that in my life, I have faced the finger and then had the Lord use me to go to that person. Yes, with each incident that has occurred with fingers in my face during my Christian walk, I eventually was led by the Spirit of the Lord to go to the people who pointed fingers at me. Did I want to go to them? Absolutely not! Sometimes it took days or weeks for me to obey the leading to do so. During this trial, there were literally years of my having to go to my brethren. This was a learning process for me.

I have two more personal tests that I want to share with you. In the first, I used to sing in a church choir, and one day during rehearsal, the choir director said she had learned that some of the choir members had been backbiting about her giving only certain people all of the lead songs. She said we should be open and speak directly if we had any feelings regarding this. Now, being the person that I am, if you ask me something, I will tell you the honest truth. God has granted me more wisdom regarding when, and when not, to impulsively speak my feelings or thoughts, and taught me not to speak just because someone has asked.

I had not made any comment to anyone beforehand about who sang lead or who didn't. It really had not

bothered me, but since she asked, I did make a suggestion that it would be nice to give this one particular
sister who had a beautiful singing voice a few more
songs to lead. The choir director stated very nicely that
this sister I mentioned was very shy, and although she
led a song or two, she really did not care to sing lead. I
was only making a suggestion, and was satisfied with
the director's answer. She was very pleasant and gave
room for discussion on this matter to others. She was
very loving and kind to all. Little did I know that my
suggestion was going to cause me to face a finger again.

I meant no harm to anyone, but know that people
may take things totally differently from the way you
intend. The aftermath of our actions demonstrates how
one can be misunderstood by others at any time, but
thank God that He sees the heart of man. After the choir
rehearsal, I was standing outside the church building,
and a very confident sister came up to me, put her finger
in my face, close to my nose, and told me God gave her
ten talents, that she was going to use them, and that
she did not care what anyone, especially me, had to say.
What is wrong with people? How could I have been so
misunderstood? I do believe my heart was in the right
place, and I had no one in particular in mind regarding
the director's statement. I was only making a suggestion. (This also helped me to learn when, and when not,
to speak.) Now, the sister who was pointing her finger
in my face has a beautiful singing voice, and evidently,
she took what was said personally. She unmistakably
thought that my suggestion was an indirect way of
saying she led too many songs. *What? Was this really
happening? Why was she thinking this and putting her
finger in my face? What is going on here?* Her interpreta-
tion was so far from what I had said. Nevertheless, she
felt invaded.

While facing the finger, of course, I stepped back—
from the uncomfortable closeness of that finger and, fur-

thermore, from the accusation. I told her, of course, she should use the talents that God had given her and that I was not directing any comment toward her or anyone in particular. This sister had allowed herself to be offended because of my suggestion. She did do the right thing by coming to me after the incident, but my, my, my, did she come boldly and with an attack-mode attitude. I was not afraid of her. She was and is a Christian, my sister in the Lord, so I did not need to fear. After praying about this and, of course, later being impressed to go to her, I called her home phone and asked if I might come over to see her. She allowed me to come, and light was shone on what had taken place when we talked. The enemy was exposed; we put him under our feet, prayed together, and were healed from what could have been coldness between us. Although we are at different churches now, we see each other here and there, and when we do, there is love and a bond between us that only God could have given. We are blessed because God healed us and truly made us whole. We are true sisters in Christ.

The third and last time I faced the finger was during a prayer time in church. A sister came up to me pointing her finger in my face, amazingly while I was walking the church floors and praying in the Holy Ghost. I saw her coming toward me with a focused look, but I really did not know why. When she reached me, she boldly placed her finger in my face and accused me of something that was absolutely not true! Since I was praying in the Holy Ghost, I thought, *Lord, what is happening here?* She had been misinformed, and I was the accused. I thought, *What is wrong with people? And why, years later, am I going through this again?* A softer approach would have been nice, wouldn't you agree, especially during prayer? Besides, I do believe I was innocent. She had been misinformed that I was the culprit. NO! NO! NO! The devil is a liar. I was sick of being accused. It was evident that she did not come to make peace, but to point the finger. Now, I do believe her deliberation was with the intention of doing right, well, and good, but I was shocked because I was facing the finger, again!

Each of the finger-in-my-face incidents occurred in different time frames. *Lord, what is this with the finger?* I'll tell you the truth: A finger in your face does not feel pleasant at all, and, of course, it is very demeaning. Because of these incidents, along with my tendency to be a peacemaker, my heart was pricked that each felt so strongly about the accusation. The fingers in my face were also in my heart, to the point that it really concerned me. One night I was awakened, and the Spirit of the Lord told me to go to the sister who had approached me while I was praying in the Holy Ghost at church. I cried so hard and asked God, "Why did it have to be me?" I was truly innocent; I had done no wrong here. "Why me, Lord?" Please, Lord, do not have me do this. Please, Lord, not with this person, not her, for it will only justify her thinking that she was right. Please, Lord, please deal with her understanding on this so she can clearly see the truth and that I was not the one to blame." God, being who He is, stood on His word to me. I cried myself to sleep. Still, as I opened my eyes the next morning, tears rolled down my face. I did not want to go to this particular sister, for she had a strong personality, so I wrote her a note indicating I was not her enemy.

> For we do not wrestle against flesh and blood, but against principalities, against powers, against the rulers of the darkness of this age, against spiritual hosts of wickedness in the heavenly places.
> Ephesians 6:12

In my note, I expressed that she was my sister in the Lord, and I asked her to forgive me if she believed in her heart that I had done her wrong. I desired to walk in the love of God, along with walking in peace with one another, not allowing the enemy to come between us. As I handed her this note, I did get a chance to speak briefly with her and tell her what the note was about, but she spoke very abruptly to me and then walked away. But, hallelujah, God, who was in charge of this, gave me some comforting words to hold on to. He also reminded me that I had done my part. I had learned from past encounters to trust Him and obey, for He will come through every time. Now, with this sister, it took some time. About two years later, early one Sunday morning before I was awake, my telephone rang. She had called to apologize for accusing me. The Lord was dealing with her concerning the past incident, and she had learned that I only *knew* of the incident she had accused me of and that I was not the perpetrator. Look at God! All three encounters were unpleasant presumptions about me surrounding misunderstandings and untruths. I believe the purpose of confrontation should be to make peace, to bring us back together again. Confrontation should not be for mere accusation, finger-pointing, and giving place to the devil.

> For unto us a Child is born, unto us a Son is given; and the government will be upon His shoulder. And His name will be called Wonderful, Counselor, Mighty God, Everlasting Father, Prince of Peace.
>
> Isaiah 9:6

God is a peacemaker, and peace is a fruit of the Spirit (Galatians 5:22). "For He Himself is our peace, who has made both one, and has broken down the middle wall of separation" (Ephesians 2:14). He would not have His children separated with walls between them. God has proved Himself again true to His Word. When you know that God has given you instructions, you can trust Him and obey Him, for He and His Word are one and the same, for He is faithful and watches over His Word to perform it.

Because of past occurrences with fingers in my face, I started wondering what the deal was with the finger-pointing. I even recalled being in junior high school in the lunchroom line when a girl put a finger in my face. I hated having a finger in my face so much that I bit hers. So I wondered, *Is this why these episodes come back to me as a Christian, to see how I will handle such situations now?* At one time, when I owned and operated a child care center. After repeatedly seeing one parent put her finger in her child's face when scolding him, I said to her nicely, "Don't do that; he has feelings." Another time I had witnessed a close family member put a finger in their child's face several times, and one day, I wanted to get a point across about the finger-pointing. After seeing this happen again, I walked up to the person, extended my finger in *that person's* face, and said, "This does not feel good in your face, does it?" With continuous shaking and pointing, I added, "Your child has feelings, just like you, so stop. It is frightening, humiliating, fear-provoking, threatening, and intimidating." Then I walked away. What is going on with people and their finger-pointing? Although this has been a test and a trial in my life that has produced wonderful testimonies and insight into God's principles, I wanted to learn more about how to deal with "the finger." The word "finger" is defined as "one of the five parts of the hand, especially the four besides the thumb." Interestingly, I also discovered that "to point the finger at" is "to single out for fault or blame, to accuse." A synonym for "accusing" is "finger-pointing." Wow! This characterization coincides with what has happened to me during the times I have faced the finger. This has given me insight, for I had never really given the finger-pointing much thought. I just knew it did not give me a pleasant feeling, and I did not like its repercussions. Learning this got my attention even more, so I decided I would search out what God had to declare about finger-pointing. Let's take a look within the Old Testament, which speaks of one's motive for fasting and also mentions finger-pointing.

> Is this not the fast that I have chosen: to loose the bonds of wickedness, to undo the heavy burdens, to let the oppressed go free, and that you break every yoke? Is it not to share your bread with the hungry, and that you bring to your house the poor who are cast out; when you see the naked, that you cover him, and not hide yourself from your own flesh? Then your light shall break forth like the morning, your healing shall spring forth speedily, and your righteousness shall go before you; the glory of the Lord shall be your rear guard. Then you shall call, and the Lord will answer; you shall cry, and He will say, "Here I am." If you take away the yoke from your midst, the pointing of the finger, and speaking wickedness . . . .
>
> Isaiah 58:6-9

God does not want fleshly, selfish motives. He does not want us to find pleasure in anything that may grieve others. Instead, He wants us "to loose the bonds of wickedness, to undo the heavy burdens, to let the oppressed go free," and to break every yoke. In doing these things, He will answer *if* you do your part, which means you must take away the yoke from your midst and cease the pointing of the finger and the speaking of wickedness. God is saying we should put away scorn, contempt, and hatred among us.

To bring forth more clarity on this, look at verse 9 from the Amplified Bible:

> Then you shall call, and the Lord will answer; you shall cry, and He will say, Here I am. If you take

away from your midst yokes of oppression [wher-
ever you find them], the finger pointed in scorn
[toward the oppressed or the godly], and every
form of false, harsh, unjust, and wicked speaking
. . . .

Isaiah 58:9 AMP

Specifically speaking, usually when someone is
pointing his or her finger, that person is bringing judgment, blame, and accusation. Earlier it was affirmed
that you should go to your brethren. The Word of God
states to go, but does not say to point the finger at your
brethren, accuse them, or blame them. Let us take
another look at that Scripture.

Moreover if your brother sins against you, go and
tell him his fault between you and him alone. If
he hears you, you have gained your brother.

Matthew 18:15

Here the Word states that "if your brother sins against
you," indicating that he first had to have done something
to offend you, then you should go and tell him what he
did. The word "fault" implies something that is not as it
should be—a defect, a mistake. To accuse or blame has
a totally different connotation, which is to hold a person
or thing responsible for something bad or wrong. This
approach is something of a fixation in the heart, and we
know that God sees and knows what is in the heart of
every person. The finger-pointing, accusing, or blaming
signifies that one holds someone or something responsible, and in doing so, there is an embrace, a grasp that
is closer to and within the heart. When it is in the heart, it
becomes a problem with God. On the other hand, Jesus
informs us how to deal with this by commissioning us
to go get things back in order. This sounds like making
peace to me. How does it sound to you? My belief is that

the person offended should go with a humble heart with the goal of restoring friendship, love, and peace. You should not have an attitude that you will beat down a person intentionally to get even with him or her. That is not God's way of doing things, for we have the love of God in our hearts. As Christians, we should know that whatever we do in word or in deed should glorify God.

> Therefore, as the elect of God, holy and beloved, put on tender mercies, kindness, humility, meekness, longsuffering; bearing with one another, and forgiving one another, if anyone has a complaint against another; even as Christ forgave you, so you also must do. But above all these things put on love, which is the bond of perfection. And let the peace of God rule in your hearts, to which also you were called in one body; and be thankful. Let the word of Christ dwell in you richly in all wisdom, teaching and admonishing one another in psalms and hymns and spiritual songs, singing with grace in your hearts to the Lord. And whatever you do in word or deed, do all in the name of the Lord Jesus, giving thanks to God the Father through Him.
>
> Colossians 3:12-17

The Christian who is being approached must also follow the Scriptures and let the character of the new born-again spirit within him or her shine. This demonstrates the love of God that indeed dwells within you. Let me point out that the Word is not instructing us to go and confront people in the world, but to go to our brethren who are in God's kingdom. His children are and should desire to be peacemakers. When we come into the knowledge of the truth of God's Word to live by, we are held accountable. We are to be doers, not hearers only, of the Word, doing our part in obedience

185

to God's Word, and not concerning ourselves with what another may or may not be doing; work out your own soul salvation with fear and trembling (Philippians 2:12). In Matthew 18:15, the word "if" is a conditional word: "If he hears you, you have gained your brother." "If he hears" implies the brother has a choice to hear or not to hear. Then, in verses 16 and 17, Jesus tells what to do if the brother chooses *not* to hear:

> But if he will not hear, take with you one or two more, that "by the mouth of two or three witnesses every word may be established." And if he refuses to hear them, tell it to the church. But if he refuses even to hear the church, let him be to you like a heathen and a tax collector.
> Matthew 18:16-17

As a parent, have you ever given your children a warning by counting one, two, three, . . . ? The child knows the number you have given him or her and how long the child has to obey or deal with the consequences. Some children will try you right up to the very last number that will bring you to discipline them. Say the number you have given the child is five, and right when you say "four," the child is up and moving. Jesus did the same thing here; He set down three steps before the fourth, which are the consequences, thereby taking action for the hardness of those who will not hear. With natural parents' children, there may be one child who comes across as stubborn and rebellious and will not budge until he or she is facing the consequences of disobedience. Assuredly, it is the same in God's family. If it should happen that His children are faced with His protocol, they really would not have to get to the last step of facing the consequences before they hear and obey, since the love of God is in their hearts. Let me use the analogy of a baseball game for you to see and understand Jesus' ruling steps: one, two, three—three strikes, and you are out (of chances to gain your brother back). This example is exactly what Jesus represented to be carried out.

Here is a breakdown of the steps in Jesus' instructions, along with His disciplinary description from Matthew 18:15-17:

Step 1: "Go and tell him his fault between you and him alone."
Step 2: "Take with you one or two more, that 'by the mouth of two or three witnesses every word may be established.'"
Step 3: "Tell it to the church."

Each one of these three steps is an action to be taken, given with the condition of "if" the brother does or does not hear. Let's look again entirely at these verses of Scripture spoken by Jesus:

Moreover *if* your brother sins against you, go and tell him his fault between you and him alone. *If* he hears you, you have gained your brother. But *if* he will not hear, take with you one or two more, that "by the mouth of two or three witnesses every word may be established." And *if* he refuses to hear them, tell it to the church. But *if* he refuses even to hear the church, let him be to you like a heathen and a tax collector.
Matthew 18:15-17 (emphasis added)

Gaining your brother, as well as having a successful end result, is what Jesus hopes for. Given the fact that all the steps, one through three, are with the condition of "if" he hears or "if" he does not hear, the choice ultimately is the brother's. If he chooses not to hear, Jesus has laid out the consequence of action to be taken, due to the chaotic behavior of a disobedient child who is not displaying the characteristics of God our Father, who is love. Only after all three steps are followed with your brother still refusing should he be like a heathen (a person who does not believe in God) and a tax collector to you. You have done all according to the words of Jesus, and your brother's heart is still hardened. The "one, two, three strikes you are out" implies that you tried to gain your brother back. You have done your part in obedience to God's Word; now leave it alone. It is evident that your brother's behavior is not reflecting God's character, and with this being so, it really should be easier not to allow yourself to be affected by it. As Christians, we do know, and also tend to understand and be more tolerant of, unbelievers' behaviors. We are more willing to leave it alone and pray for them, yet we are sometimes not willing to do the same when it comes to believers.

Let me specify that Jesus did not say your brother was a heathen, but that he should "be to you like a heathen and a tax collector." Now you are enlightened and able to have compassion for your brother as one who needs Jesus, as do all people, believers and unbelievers alike. A healing should take place in your heart, and you should not hold a grudge or feel resentment toward your brother. We, the family of God, for the most part will not experience all the conditional steps. More than likely, an issue will be resolved during step 1. God our Father, like any concerned parent, gives out orderly instructions to be carried out for the reason of keeping out conflict, strife, and division within the family unit. Any loving parent will desire peace and harmony in his or her household, instead of having a home troubled with strife, bitterness, animosity, resentment, and malice.

Jesus has told us how to solve offenses, and we should be obedient to the Word given to us and not brush it aside as if nothing has happened. If this happens to occur in the local body, ordinarily, a mature Christian will hear you as well as receive you. Every born-again Christian should be sensitive to the righteous side of things, knowing right from wrong and having a tender heart to make amends. No one really wants to feel the pain of any hurt caused by someone, but how the person deals with it is another factor that will show somehow what is on the inside of the person. What is in a man will come out. Even those we know as the more spiritual Christians can sometimes seem cold toward the brethren. Is that God? I think not. Check your heart, and be honest with yourself. Examine your heart, and see what's there toward a Christian who may have done you wrong. How it can be ignored and you be okay with Jesus is far beyond my understanding. People may fool people, but one thing is for sure: God knows what is really in the heart of man, and He cannot be fooled. With Jesus' constructive teaching, we will be more profitable in our lives by withdrawing from things that put up walls between us. We say we want the glory of God to fall, so let's get things right and our hearts clear. God wants His people liberated from wrongdoing, and through exercising the Word of God in our lives, we will set in position an avenue of helping to set people free. God has a way of dealing with the matters of the heart of man, in addition to the finger-pointing, which apparently is also an issue of the heart.

To learn more about references to finger-pointing in the Word of God, let's look at events related to the power of the pointing finger that concern Jesus Himself. In the first instance, He was casting out a demon, and some of the multitude thought that Jesus was being assisted by Beelzebub, the devil. Now, how could they possibly think that Jesus needed help casting out a devil? And why would the devil help Jesus to cast out his own kind? Anyone can see that this does not make sense. Here is what happens:

> And He was casting out a demon, and it was mute. So it was, when the demon had gone out, that the mute spoke; and the multitudes marveled. But some of them said, "He casts out demons by Beelzebub, the ruler of the demons." Others, testing Him, sought from Him a sign from heaven. But He, knowing their thoughts, said to them: "Every kingdom divided against itself is brought to desolation, and a house divided against a house falls. If Satan also is divided against himself, how will his kingdom stand? Because you say I cast out demons by Beelzebub. And if I cast out demons by Beelzebub, by whom do your sons cast them out? Therefore they will be your judges. But if I cast out demons with the finger of God, surely the kingdom of God has come upon you."
>
> Luke 11:14-20

Believers should not even think or ask if Jesus needed or wanted help from a devil. Thinking so is like saying Jesus had no authority over a devil and needed help from the weakest link, the devil, to cast out another devil. How contrary and far from the truth! Jesus is Lord of lords and King of kings, and He needs no help from a devil. Jesus said in verse 20, "But if I cast out demons with the finger of God, surely the kingdom of God has come upon you" (indicating that if the kingdom of God has for sure come upon them, they, too, can cast out the devil). He informed them that when they stood with Him, they were strong, and helped them to understand that a house divided cannot stand. Jesus also stated:

> When a strong man, fully armed, guards his own palace, his goods are in peace. But when a

stronger than he comes upon him and overcomes him, he takes from him all his armor in which he trusted, and divides his spoils. He who is not with Me is against Me, and he who does not gather with Me scatters.

Luke 11:21-23

Jesus had given them an example whereby they might choose whose side they were going to be on. The stronger one—Jesus—comes with the capability, power, and authority to overcome the lesser, the weakest link— the devil. Just imagine Jesus pointing His finger and casting the devil out. The devil had to obey (leave), for the finger of God, the stronger and greater One, had pointed at him. God is always accurate. When He points His finger in accusation or judgment, He is not going to miss the mark. The devil had been accused, and rightfully so, for he had caused someone to be in a mute state, which is not of God. Nor is it the best state for anyone to be in. With that being said, pointing the finger at the devil is well and good because he is to blame for anything that is not like God—any lack, sickness, disease, and most definitely any faulty out-of-order doings among believers, such as discord, lack of harmony, or conflict, resulting in division.

Beyond the natural comprehension of man, God's wisdom, followed, will lead to a wonderful outcome. When we are tested or accused by anyone, we can always examine and follow the example provided by Jesus when the scribes, along with the Pharisees, came to test and accuse Him. Jesus was slow to speak, but when He did, He did not point the finger directly at anyone. He placed His finger to the ground during His test. Let's look closer and really observe how they tested Jesus when they brought him a woman caught in the act of adultery. By bringing her to Him, they already were symbolically pointing the finger, accusing her, blaming her. They hoped that Jesus would agree with them regarding an inaccurate quote of the Law of Moses so they could go a step further with their intention to accuse Him. The test they gave Jesus was in the question they asked him concerning the Law of Moses. Jesus was teaching the people when this interruption impolitely came, with no consideration of the importance of His teachings and the people in the audience, who were learning. In addition to its being rude, it showed that they really did not care about the importance of Jesus' teachings or the people who were learning from Him. Of course, they did not think Jesus was sent by or knew God. Their only purpose in coming was to test and to accuse Jesus. They only wanted an accusation and a judgment. Accusation and judgment were exactly what they received, only not in the way they anticipated. Now, remember that finger-pointing often means accusing.

> But Jesus went to the Mount of Olives. Now early in the morning He came again into the temple, and all the people came to Him; and He sat down and taught them. Then the scribes and Pharisees brought to Him a woman caught in adultery. And when they had set her in the midst, they said to Him, "Teacher, this woman was caught in adultery, in the very act. Now Moses, in the law, commanded us that such should be stoned. But what do You say?" This they said, testing Him, that they might have something of which to accuse Him. But Jesus stooped down and wrote on the ground with His finger, as though He did not hear. So when they continued asking Him, He raised Himself up and said to them, "He who is without sin among you, let him throw a stone at her first." And again He stooped down and wrote on the ground. Then those who heard it, being convicted by their conscience, went out

one by one, beginning with the oldest even to the last. And Jesus was left alone, and the woman standing in the midst. When Jesus had raised Himself up and saw no one but the woman, He said to her, "Woman, where are those accusers of yours? Has no one condemned you?" She said, "No one, Lord." And Jesus said to her, "Neither do I condemn you; go and sin no more."

John 8:1-11

The scribes and Pharisees first and foremost wanted to accuse Jesus. They knew the law they referred to did not specifically say to stone the woman, but they obviously did not think Jesus knew accurately what the law said, and they hoped they could find justifiable grounds to possibly stone Him. Have you heard the saying that when you point one finger at someone, you have three pointing back at you? The scribes' and Pharisees' actions brought exactly this upon them. They had interrupted Jesus' teachings. They passed judgment and then, when faced with their own sins, did not have a clear conscience in judging another. In order to accuse Jesus, they used Scripture taken out of context from the Law of Moses. Now, what they said and carried out was different from what the Scripture says. You probably have heard the saying, "Actions speak louder than words." I periodically say it's in the "do." (You truly can watch more of what people do than what they say.) Let's look at what they quoted, along with what the Old Testament alleges.

They said to Him, "Teacher, this woman was caught in adultery, in the very act. Now Moses, in the law, commanded us that such should be stoned. But what do You say?"

John 8:4-5

The man who commits adultery with another man's wife, he who commits adultery with his neighbor's wife, the adulterer and the adulteress, shall surely be put to death.

Leviticus 20:10

If a man is found lying with a woman married to a husband, then both of them shall die—the man that lay with the woman, and the woman; so you shall put away the evil from Israel.

Deuteronomy 22:22

Certainly, if the scribes' and Pharisees' intentions were truly meant to be in obedience to the law, then shouldn't they have brought both the man and the woman to Jesus? So where was the man? Did they just let him go? How was it possible for them to catch her in the very act without a man being there in the act, too? Was the man caught in the very act with the woman among them as they brought the woman to Jesus, perhaps part of the plot that they had conjured up to test Jesus? WHERE was he? Did they let him go and just grab the woman? Did they really plot and plan in a scheme "with the man" caught in the very act? Matthew 12:14...the Pharisees went out and plotted against Him, how they might destroy Him. Possibly they guaranteed they would let the man off the hook of shame. Again, WHERE was he? No matter the speculation, the man caught in the very act with the woman was not presented with her. What we do know from looking at the Scripture is that both were not offered for the judgment. Only one was presented to Jesus—the woman.

The Scripture in Leviticus specifically indicates that "the adulterer and the adulteress, shall surely be put to death." In the book of Deuteronomy, it clearly states that they shall "both" die—"the man that lay with the woman, and the woman." So obviously, their motive was not to act as the Law of Moses plainly specified. What is evident without doubt is their intention to set Jesus up so they could accuse Him of stoning only the woman.

Oh, they were very aware of what they were doing. Scribes were men who knew the laws to the letter and taught the law. They purposely chose to speak a half truth of a known law, thus testing Jesus to see if He knew the truth. As an association, the Pharisees were a society of zealously religious men who acted under the scribes' guidance in opposition to the godless, which is what they thought Jesus was.

The scribes and Pharisees agreed to use their superiority and influence and approached Jesus during a time of His teaching. With their fabrication, they hoped to persuade all who were in the audience that Jesus was not of God. They had interrupted Jesus' teachings, and set the woman caught in adultery directly in the midst of Jesus and the spectators, waiting for Jesus to pass judgment. They waited like a pack of wolves in sheep's clothing with anticipation for His response to their inaccurate reference to the Law of Moses.

They knew the correct answer when they asked Jesus this test question: "But what do You say?" This reminds me of taking tests in school. Sometimes the questions were worded in a way that could trick you into giving the wrong answer. But if you studied the homework assignment thoroughly, no matter how the question was worded, you knew the correct answer. Jesus knew the answer, and knew the intent and motives of the hearts of the questioners. So wisely, instead of pointing His finger openly at anyone, especially at the woman caught in the very act, Jesus stooped down and placed His finger to the ground and wrote, which *implied* accusation. Jesus Himself did not verbally accuse anyone of anything, but the scribes and Pharisees persisted in asking Him, determined to get His response.

Unmistakably, they really did not know, nor were they willing to accept, that Jesus was the true Son of God, sent from God, and furthermore that He knew all things. You have to love the Lord for His wisdom. Jesus knew how to stop them in their little scheme by means of a straightforward statement that He made that subsequently placed the judgment upon them, concluding the issue. Jesus had the final say; He was in right standing, without sin. Furthermore, He would not have cast a stone at the woman caught in the very act of adultery because when He judges, He judges rightfully. Jesus knew the whole truth that both the man and woman caught in the very act of adultery were not present, and more importantly, He also knew the scribes' and Pharisees' objective was to have Him destroyed. But His time had not yet come.

It is important that you continually read the Bible to grow and become knowledgeable in the Word of God so you will know truth in order to apply it in your everyday life and not be deceived by the enemy's devices. We have heard it said that the truth will make you free, but accurately, Jesus says:

> If you abide in My word, you are My disciples indeed. And you shall know the truth, and the truth shall make you free.
>
> John 8:31-32

We see here again the word "if" as a conditional word, giving the stipulation that you do your part and "abide" in the Word or, as some translations articulate, that you "continue in" the word," and then "truth shall make you free."

People have come to me sharing what someone has done to them. Along with, obviously, hearing their hurt, I heard their heartfelt concern. I was able to detect their bitterness and resentment, and I know what Jesus has to say on the matter and also believe that this really is a heart issue. I advised them to go in love to the person they were speaking of to make peace. It really amazes me how many people are afraid or do not care to confront others, but they carry a wound and pain with a bitterness in their hearts. Saying what they are feeling is an indication that the bitter root is in their heart toward their brother or sister in Christ. God sees what is in the heart, and it is the heart that must be dealt with. This bitterness is something that should not be in people of Christ because it can eat them up on the inside like gangrene if it is not dealt with properly. People's hearts and eyes should be open to activating God's Word and to doing what God wants. In His family, God wants peace. He wants the walls down, with no division, or separation, among the members of His family. So we must get rid of any blemishes within, the conflicts and resistance to the will of God, for the sake of being in one accord. Some may say that because of their personality, they will not go and speak with someone in order to make peace. Be aware of the feelings in your heart toward the person. Besides, the Word of God has not been distributed in part according to personalities, to a select few. The Word is for all who would read, study, hear, partake, and be doers, for it is relevant that we are walking in love. God is love! We are to be doers, not just hearers, of the Word of God.

> If someone says, "I love God," and hates his brother, he is a liar; for he who does not love his brother whom he has seen, how can he love God whom he has not seen? And this commandment we have from Him: that he who loves God must love his brother also.
>
> 1 John 4:20-21

Perhaps the hesitancy to do what the Word of God says could stem from a fear of not having a successful outcome—a fear of being hurt, a fear of persecution, a fear of not being liked, or a fear of a fight. But wait a minute. We know that fear is not of God, and we do not have to be afraid. Fear is what stops one from doing what should be done. Fear is false evidence appearing real. Fear is of the devil and not of God. Some may even say that they are walking in love by choosing to ignore when a brother or sister has offended them. There's no reason to go to your brother or sister if your heart is clear and you really have not taken any offense. If you see that your brother or sister has not sinned against you and your heart holds no grudge or resentment toward him or her, and you are not treating the person differently by not walking in love with him or her or causing the person hurt due to any behavior change toward him or her, then there are no grounds to go to that person. Many years ago, I used to hear my former pastor say to the congregation, "All hearts clear." It's really about the heart, and without a doubt if your heart is clear, then clear it is. Praise God, for He has given us His Holy Spirit to lead and guide us, along with His Word. As the body of Christ, the believing Christians, we are expected to be in obedience to the written and spoken words of God. Enough with all the excuses, the personality types, and the phobia about taking responsibility; just do what the Word of God says, for the Word of God works far better than any man's feelings or theories. Apply the Word of God in your life; just "do it," and whatever the "it" is for you, know that it's the "do" that gets "it" done. You often will hear me state, "Father knows best"—meaning our heavenly Father, the one and only true God, the Master and King, the omniscient One who knows everything and what's best suitable for every situation. Believers should not defy or disregard His instructions, for it pays to adhere to what has been said to the church, the body of Christ.

Jesus was not speaking to unbelievers, but to the believers when He made mention of dealing with a brother. He does not mention that believing Christians are to go out and confront people of the world who are outside of the body, but those within the body. Jesus gave further instructions because of the hardness of some people's hearts, the state or level in which they may find themselves. Jesus has said that after you go and tell your brother his fault, between the two of you alone, if he hears you, you have gained your brother and harmony shall be replaced. But perhaps your brother does not hear. In that case, Jesus said:

> But if he will not hear, take with you one or two more, that "by the mouth of two or three witnesses every word may be established." And if he refuses to hear them, tell it to the church. But if he refuses even to hear the church, let him be to you like a heathen and a tax collector.
>
> Matthew 18:16-17

Jesus knows that taking the next step of taking two or three with you will provide witnesses to every word in case he still refuses to hear you. (It sounds like rebellion if a person continues not to hear you.) There are people who will not budge because to them, it is like admitting to the wrongdoing or not wanting to humble themselves by apologizing. Let's face it, no one really wants to be wrong about anything, but it happens to all of us. We miss it at times, but knowingly or unknowingly, we sometimes are just outright wrong. We are imperfect beings striving for that maturity in the body of Christ. We may be aware or unaware of hurting or wronging someone; however, the fact remains that if a person comes and accuses you of wronging him or her, even if you believe you are innocent, you need to put on some humility and reach out to help mend a broken heart by walking in the love of God. Embrace righteousness instead of looking at it from a selfish standpoint and refusing to hear and give your brother peace and harmony. You may feel he or she is taking offense or being too touchy, which may be so, but do the Christian thing, and walk in love for the healing of hearts. Comfort the person, for this may be a test of your obedience to God's Word.

The test: Being approached with finger-pointing (accusations) and how to handle it.

The trial: The examination of the heart and what's in it.

The testimony: A doer of the Word of God, loving the brethren and not pointing the finger. Walls are torn down within the family of God, and walking in peace and harmony.

Pray this prayer: *Father, I ask You for wisdom as I exercise walking in the fruit of the Spirit of love. Establish my heart with compassion manifested in my life toward my brothers and sisters in Christ Jesus. Forgive me of any judgment or grief that I may have bestowed upon another; work and stir my heart with maturity to see as You see the brethren. In the course of my faith activated, I am rooted and grounded in love, that I am able to comprehend with all the saints what is the width and length and depth and height, to know the love of Christ, which passes knowledge, that I am being filled with all the fullness of God. I thank You, Father, who "is able to do exceedingly abundantly above" all that I ask or think, according to the power that works in me. Be glorified in the church and through me as I take hold of Your Word. In Jesus' name I pray. Amen.*

So then, each of us will give account of
ourselves to God. Therefore let us stop passing
judgement on one another. Instead, make up
your mind not to put any stumbling block
or obstacle in the way of a brother or sister.
Romans 14:12-13 NIV

Trusting and Letting Go

Trust in the Lord with all your heart, and lean not
on your own understanding.

Proverbs 3:5

If you ask most Christians if they trust God, depend
on God, believe in God, rely on God, or have faith
in God, most likely their answer will be yes, they do
trust God. Trust implies that one has a firm belief in
the honesty, truthfulness, justice, or power of a person
or thing. It means you feel you can totally depend on
and lean on that person or entity with faith and confidence. A person who says, "I once trusted someone" is
probably thinking about a previous trust that failed and
caused hurt. "Trusting" is not a past-tense word, in that
you let it, in itself, go, but it is a word that continues the
path of the word "trust."

The Lord dealt with me regarding trusting and letting go for about two years before I really trusted Him
and learned how to let go. One day while at my office, I
heard, "Trust Me," and I said, "I trust You, Lord." Then
came, "You think you trust Me." Another day I heard
again, "Trust Me." I responded, again, "I trust You,
Lord," and for a second time I heard, "You think you
trust Me." Another day, once again I heard, "Trust Me,
Pat," to which I said, "Lord, You know I trust You," and
again, for the third time, I heard, "You think you trust

Me." I felt like Peter when Jesus asked him three times if he loved Him while showing Himself to His disciples after His Resurrection:

> So when they had eaten breakfast, Jesus said to Simon Peter, "Simon, son of Jonah, do you love Me more than these?" He said to Him, "Yes, Lord; You know that I love You." He said to him, "Feed My lambs." He said to him again a second time, "Simon, son of Jonah, do you love Me?" He said to Him, "Yes, Lord; You know that I love you." He said to him, "Tend My sheep." He said to him the third time, "Simon, son of Jonah, do you love Me?" Peter was grieved because He said to him the third time, "Do you love Me?" And he said to Him, "Lord, You know all things; You know that I love You." Jesus said to him, "Feed My sheep."
>
> John 21:15-17

Like Peter, Lord, You know all things. After hearing this from the Lord, I must admit, I also got a little agitated after hearing three times, "Trust Me," and following my reply that I did trust Him, "You think you trust Me." Because I heard no more than that, I asked God, "Why am I being asked to trust You?"

I heard absolutely nothing, not a word, so my solution was to take this in prayer and pray it through, not really knowing that a task was ahead of me that would entail the extent of my obeying, trusting, and letting go. Praying another day, I heard the Spirit of the Lord say to me, "Sell out to me." I continued to pray and told God that my heart was sold out to Him: "I am sold out to You. I love You with all my heart, my soul, and my mind." My thought was, *Isn't that being sold out?* It was later I came to realize that God was directing me to sell my business, to come home from the workforce, and pray, and then the trust issue was on. "God, my business is my bread and butter, and besides, I know I have read in the Bible, "If anyone will not work, neither shall he eat" (2 Thessalonians 3:10). Periodically, I would reason in my heart to sell out my business and come home.

Sadly, it took me some time (about two years) to trust and let go of what I thought was my security. After I signed the contract, selling my business, I went home and fell on my knees. I cried out to God, saying, "Lord, what have I done?" I heard in my spirit, "Now, I know that you love Me," and I responded, "Lord, didn't You know that before?" I asked God to take care of me because I did not like depending on anyone. Once, I told God I did not want to come home and depend on Mike, my husband, and I heard, "You are not to depend on Mike, but depend on Me." Would you believe that out of my mouth came, "Lord, your timing is not my timing," which indicated that in my heart, I did not even want to depend on God when it came to finances and taking care of me? I did not look to or depend on anyone when it came to taking care of me. If I needed something, I had to do something to obtain it. I did not like depending on anyone. I knew myself, and I knew that if something needed to be done for myself, I would be getting it done. I had learned not to look to anyone for anything, that most people are concerned with themselves. God knows what's in the heart of a person, and it is the heart that must be dealt with. I did not know then that my issue was independence; I just questioned, *Whom could I depend on but me to take care of me?* I had done it so long that I didn't know how to look to anyone for anything. This was a deep-rooted issue that God knew about me, and He later revealed why I had a problem with trusting people. He alone was and is my Refuge, my Helper, the One you and I are to depend on in everything.

Can you recall the Spirit of the Lord speaking to you in response to your thoughts when you were merely thinking something but had not said a word, especially when your thoughts were in connection to His words that were previously spoken to you? This is the Spirit of the Lord, indicating that He is a discerner of the very thoughts and intents of the heart.

> For the word of God is living and powerful, and sharper than any two-edged sword, piercing even to the division of soul and spirit, and of joints and marrow, and is a discerner of the thoughts and intents of the heart.
>
> Hebrews 4:12

God is omniscient, and there is nothing hidden from Him, not our thoughts or actions. There is no place to hide. One night while I was sitting in church, in my heart and still working within me came the words, "Trust Me." I glanced at my husband, Mike, sitting next to me and had the thought that I didn't want to depend on him. I heard clearly, "Get your eyes off of Mike." Then I heard, "I am going to deliver you from your independence." God knew my thoughts and the intent of my heart, that they were full of the desire for self-reliance. His intent was that I trust and depend totally on Him.

God wants His children to trust Him, to totally rely on, depend on, and have confidence in Him and not trust our own intellectual understanding. When you have let go of your own understanding, of trying to fix things physically or mentally regarding whatever it may be that you are holding on to, it's a good indicator that you are trusting God. God's ways are higher than our ways, and it takes the God kind of faith to surrender and completely trust Him and let go. When you trust God, everything will turn out to be all right, regardless of what may be going on in the natural realm. It's easy to say that you trust God when things are going well; it's when those things turn sour that you may feel it's a bit challenging to trust Him. The economy may look bleak, your finances may be limited, bills are due, children are gone astray, and life appears to be hopeless. Don't be dismayed and lose heart, but hold on. Roll your cares over on the Lord, and let Him carry the weight for you. Keep trusting in Him. Even when you cannot see an immediate change, don't stop trusting. Trusting God regardless of the circumstances will cause you to reap a harvest if you faint not. Don't allow your life to be entangled by what's going on around you because all things eventually change. Besides, the things that are seen are temporary, meaning they are subject to change. So trust God, because change is coming!

> . . . while we do not look at the things which are seen, but at the things which are not seen. For the things which are seen are temporary, but the things which are not seen are eternal.
>
> 2 Corinthians 4:18

The things that you see are temporary, and surely they will pass. Take up trust; relax and enter the peace of God with belief and expectation, and you will see in the end the results will turn out in your favor. Hand over and detach from your limitations. Learn to entrust your life to the only One capable of getting the job done, God. Even employers are known to hand over and delegate particular responsibilities to trustworthy employees who can carry out given job descriptions. An employer is not worried or concerned if the employee is going to get the job done because the employer trusts him or her. He or she has confidence and the expectation that the job will get done. Therefore, the employer releases himself or herself from doing a task, and hands it over to another person. The employer totally surrenders and lets go of the task, giving it to the employee, with no worry, but trusting and relying on someone else to take on the responsibility. That's trust. God, your heavenly Father, knows best, and He wants you to cast all your cares, worries, and concerns over onto Him, for He cares for you. He is a big God with strong shoulders to hold much more than you can ever carry.

> For unto us a Child is born, unto us a Son is given; and the government will be upon His shoulder. And His name will be called Wonderful, Counselor, Mighty God, Everlasting Father, Prince of Peace.
> Isaiah 9:6

The fact that His shoulder is strong enough to have the government upon it helps us to see that our cares are but small in comparison. Go on and do it—hand over your cares. Besides, worrying will only make you have stress and anxiety that can build to depression, sickness, and disease. All of these things are traps of the enemy, so cast all your cares upon Him, and let Him carry them for you. It will take the burdens off you. If you have to, literally get up, walk away from your troubles, and refocus in another direction. Deliberately set your mind on something else. Read the Bible or a good book, listen to music, go out for fresh air and sunshine, visit a relative or friend, or watch a comedy, for "a merry heart [laughter] does good, like medicine" (Proverbs 17:22). Sitting around moping, sad and gloomy, is not going to fix anything, so why give in to it? Discipline yourself to move in another direction. Don't give in to negative thoughts. If you catch yourself doing so, simply say, "I will trust God and let go." There is nothing too big for God to handle. No matter the particular situation, it's always best to trust and put your confidence and faith in God. In the beginning of my marriage, I worked outside the home, although my husband always wanted me to be at home. I couldn't see that at the time, of course, due to my being "independent me."

In 1998, the Lord dealt with my heart to buy my mother a car. I thought, *Is this God?* I thought I would be able to push it from my spirit, thinking that this was coming from my head in my natural thinking. I went into reasoning mode, questioning: "God, why should I do this? Buy her a car? Is this really you? Why not a car for myself?" After I shared this with my husband, we both agreed to obey God and buy her a car. God through us showed my mom, more of His love. Whenever any family member, including herself, was in need of prayer, she called me to pray. While I was in the hospital waiting room with other family members before her surgery, a nurse came and called my name. My mother had sent for me and a nurse led me to her in a holding room where she waited before being taken in for surgery. At that time, the hospital had not administered any anesthetic to reduce or prevent pain; therefore, she was in great pain as she waited. She took hold of my arm and cried out, saying "Tricia (the name the family calls me), help me." I laid my hand on her and said, "In the name of Jesus, I command this pain to leave, right now!"

My mom breathed a deep sigh, lay back, and relaxed. The pain had instantaneously left her. A few minutes later, she was calling the names of people who were gone from this life—her twin sister and her mother. I knew in my heart that she was going to be with Jesus soon. I said, "Mom, call on Jesus," and then she called on the name of the Lord. My mom had told me to release her and let her go, confirming what the Spirit of the Lord had told me the same day. I began to minister to her about her heart being clear and her being ready to go be with Jesus. Soon after that, the hospital staff came to take her for surgery. She went home to be with the Lord a week to the day after her surgery. God did not *take* my mother. She willed herself to go. She was tired of the fight to live. She knew that my prayers were holding her, and asked me to release and let her go. I am thankful she knew the love of God. She knew God answered prayers; she really believed in prayer. God had used me as a conduit to minister to her on many occasions. Trusting God to do what you cannot do has great rewards. As He knows all things, God knew that my mom would be leaving us in November 2002. Six months before, in May, I had made the last payment on the new car purchased for her. It's vital to be in obedience to the leading of the Holy Spirit. Trust God, and let go of your own preconceived thoughts about how something should be done or take place. God knows the outcome of all things; therefore, trust Him and let go.

When I was led to come home from the workplace, I had tests and trials. I often wanted to go back to work. My independence was calling on me again, and I was in danger of falling into the snare of my mind. The economy was hurting, which affected my husband's business. Lord, he needs help. Hello, drum roll please, here comes the spirit of the helpmate in me getting in the way with this thought: "I can HELP." Besides, this is my opportunity to go back where I belong, the workplace. After I told him I wanted to get a job and help him, my husband still said, "I need you to be at home." I did not understand why he felt this way. Since I was the one handling the bills, I could see he needed help with finances coming in. No one was freely handing out money to us, and besides, isn't it necessary to take up the slack? I did not understand why my husband, who needed help, would not let me help him. Was it his pride? What was wrong with him? So I persisted in asking him about my going back to work until one day, my husband said to me, "Go ahead, if that's what you want to do." I was happy and excited, and felt released to pursue a job. One day, while I was going to a place of business to put in an application, as I walked toward the office, I heard the Spirit of the Lord say to me, "Where do you think you are going?" I knew He was restraining me, but I responded, "Lord, my husband has released me." Then I heard, "That was only because of your persistence; it is not his heart." I turned around, went back to my vehicle, and went home. That encounter reminded me of what the Lord had said to me a few years earlier, that He was going to deliver me from my independence. This made me realize I had given in to what things looked like. I had stepped away from faith and trust in God, so I had to repent, trust God for all our needs, and let go of the cares. Sometimes when you trust and let go, it appears that you have lost control, which makes it easy for you to get in the way. When you know God has given you a word, don't shift gears. Stay with what He has said. With much prayer, praise, and worship, you will have a breakthrough, just as we did. God is faithful when you let go and trust Him, for His ways are higher than our ways. We must not allow our feelings to get in the way of the will of God. Where has the Holy Spirit led you? Are you fixated to it? Have you taken a detour away from it? If so, get back on track to the will of God that you know He has for you, and be watchful not to be devoured.

Be sober, be vigilant; because your adversary the devil walks about like a roaring lion, seeking whom he may devour.

1 Peter 5:8

Are you going to let the devil devour you? You have willpower in the matter. "May" is a permissible word meaning you allow something to happen. If you have ever watched a show about the animal kingdom, you've noticed how the lions go after the smallest, most vulnerable ones that have walked or wandered away from the safety of the group, their protection. Once a young animal wanders away from his pride, he, too, becomes prey. Will you walk away from that which God has given you to become vulnerable and devoured? Will you trust God and His Word for you? Will you let go of your way of doing things? Proverbs 3:5 tells us, "Trust in the Lord with all your heart"—not with some of it, not with a little of it, or even with most of your heart, but with ALL your heart. Trusting with "all your heart" means you have given everything over to Him without trying to figure it all out on your own. God wants to protect your heart from all the junk and issues of life that want to filter their way into your heart, contrary to Him. God looks at the condition of the heart. The heart is who you are in reality; it's vitally important to God. "For as he thinks in his heart, so is he" (Proverbs 23:7). God wants *all* of who you are. *All* means everything, the whole, in its entirety, which leaves nothing available for anything else. If someone gave you all of his or her pie, cake, or even all the person's possessions, there is nothing left over for that person to give to anyone else because he or she gave it all to you. Giving all your heart to God says your heart has nothing left over to give elsewhere since He has it all. You are carefree when you trust God with all your heart. You have let go. You will be all right in His care.

Sometimes trust can be misplaced, such as when you trust a spouse, children, pastor, doctor, lawyer, friend, employer, or your accountant more than God. I am not saying people are not trustworthy, only that with all your heart, you can and should trust God. It may be a fact that you have been given results by a medical doctor, a diagnosis of something that is not good, possibly a terminal report, but that is not the final say on the matter. No! That might be a fact, but it is not the truth. Trust the Word of God on the matter. His Word is true.

Surely He has borne our griefs and carried our sorrows; yet we esteemed Him stricken . . . . But

He was wounded for our transgressions, He was bruised for our iniquities; the chastisement for our peace was upon Him, and by His stripes we are healed.

Isaiah 53:4-5

So whose reports are you going to believe, God's or men's? God's, of course, for His Word is Spirit and is life that overrides man's word whenever it contradicts what His report says. Whenever you hear anything that's contrary to the Word of God, intercept it and speak the Word of God, for He has the final say. For this reason, you can trust Him with all your heart and lean not on your own understanding. God "is able to do exceedingly abundantly above all that we ask or think, according to the power that works in us" (Ephesians 3:20).

So shall My word be that goes forth out of My mouth: it shall not return to Me void [without producing any effect, useless], but it shall accomplish that which I please and purpose, and it shall prosper in the thing for which I sent it.

Isaiah 55:11 AMP

The only way that anything is voided is if it is not being utilized. When we speak the Word of God, it's being utilized, and therefore, it's not voided. More to the point, God watches over His Word "to perform it" (Jeremiah 1:12, AMP), and in the New Testament tells us His Word is "alive and active" (Hebrews 4:12, NIV).

Call on what you want in life, not what you have, and speak those things that are not as though they were. What is it you need? Call it! If your children are outside playing, or even your pets, you know they are there, although you may not physically see them. You "call" them with the expectation of their coming. Whatever you "call" will answer you. Are you calling and speaking your problems—or the answers? Speak the answers; call on what you want, not what you have. Faith-filled words have power to bring things into existence.

> (As it is written, "I have made you a father of many nations") in the presence of Him whom he believed—God, who gives life to the dead and calls those things which do not exist as though they did; who, contrary to hope, in hope believed, so that he became the father of many nations, according to what was spoken, "So shall your descendants be."
>
> Romans 4:17-18

> And since we have the same spirit of faith, according to what is written, "I believed and therefore I spoke," we also believe and therefore speak.
>
> 2 Corinthians 4:13

You can locate yourself in what you truly believe by what you are speaking. Are you holding on to what you see instead of letting God handle it, or meditating and speaking the Word of God over your circumstances? Walking by faith is having substance in that for which you are hoping. What material are you using to show your faith? Speaking the Word of God is good substance. You may have set goals and put forth physical effort to cause change in some areas in your life. Are you waiting for a giggly, gushy feeling? Or are you confident in the faithfulness of God? He is the Wisdom, the Help you need to bring what you desire to pass. Everything we see and feel is not alone in what is real. As a matter of fact, things are first in the spiritual realm before they are manifested in the natural realm. We believe that God is real and that He does exist, yet we don't see Him in the natural, for He is Spirit. People do many things in faith before they see the reality of them, such as working forty hours a week with the belief they will get a paycheck they have not yet seen; getting in their car, putting the key in the ignition, and believing they can drive off in it, trusting that it will go; sitting in a chair because they believe it will hold them; paying money for a ticket to fly on an airplane that they have not seen; and flying on the plane to get from one state to another without checking or inquiring about its safety. The things that are not seen by the natural eye are just as real as things you are able to see with the natural eye. The things you hope for are the things you do not physically see, and those are the things you are to "call" on. You are to "call" for that which is good, for God brings about goodness and not evil.

Every good gift and every perfect gift is from above, and comes down from the Father of lights, with whom there is no variation or shadow of turning.
James 1:17

God is always good. He does not deviate from goodness, nor is there a smidgen of Him turning from it. So should you hear anyone saying God had something to do with bad or evil things happening to him or her, or on this earth, don't believe it. It's not God, for He is always good. So when things appear to be hard to deal with or not happening as fast as you would like them to, stay with God, and continue to trust Him.

Do you run and hide when things don't go your way? Are you quick to give in to fits, outbursts, or tantrums when struggling with circumstances, your life, and the people in it? Instead, you should humble yourself before God, and take Him at His Word. Are you practicing self-control, and will you allow the Holy Spirit to be your umpire? Will you trust God and let go of things that bind and want to devour you? Or are you giving permission to life's circumstances or others to predict your outcome? Examine yourself, making sure you are really trusting God and letting go of whatever things that try to hold you captive to them. Keep things in proper perspective, and you will see God arise and your enemy scatter.

The test: Trusting God with all your heart and not leaning on your own understanding.

The trial: Waiting patiently regardless of life's circumstances.

The testimony: Walking by faith, not by sight, living carefree, trusting, and having let go of things that can hinder or hold me back. God supply's all my needs according to His riches in glory by Christ Jesus.

Pray this prayer: *Father, I am thankful that You are there, that I may trust in You. I ask You to bring Your Word to my remembrance, that I may speak Your Word only when all odds seem to be against me. Help me to know Your will, and trust that You will come through for me. You are faithful, and I know I can depend on You. Father, I will trust You with all my heart and not lean on my own understanding. My help comes from You, and I ask You to help me take You at Your Word, knowing that You are not a man and that You would not lie. Thank You for being my Source of help, the One in whom I put my trust. Keep me in all my ways as I continually acknowledge You. In Jesus' name I pray. Amen.*

Trust in the Lord with all your heart,
And lean not on your own understanding;
In all your ways acknowledge Him,
And He shall direct your paths.
Proverbs 3:5-6

Renewing the Mind

And do not be conformed to this world, but be transformed by the renewing of your mind, that you may prove what is that good and acceptable and perfect will of God.

Romans 12:2

Being a born-again believer alone is not enough to live and have a victorious life. Our mind has to be renewed from its old way of thinking, and the way to renew it is through the Word of God. "Renew" means to make new again; make like new, to restore or renovate in good condition. The Word of God would not have told us to renew our mind if it did not need to be renewed. When believers get saved, it's the spirit man that is born again, and not the mind and the flesh. For someone to be born again, there has to have been a first birth. Jesus tells of the two, one being a physical birth, and the other a spiritual birth.

Jesus answered and said to him, "Most assuredly, I say to you, unless one is born again, he cannot see the kingdom of God." Nicodemus said to Him, "How can a man be born when he is old? Can he enter a second time into his mother's womb and be born?" Jesus answered, "Most assuredly, I say to you, unless one is born of water and the

Spirit, he cannot enter the kingdom of God. That which is born of the flesh is flesh, and that which is born of the Spirit is spirit. Do not marvel that I said to you, 'You must be born again.'"

John 3:3-7

When the Bible speaks of being "born of water," it is speaking about the physical birth, not a baptism. The "second" birth is a spiritual birth, which means to be born of the "Spirit," God's Holy Spirit. Without being born again, man's natural mind cannot understand the things of God, and to do so, he must be born again spiritually to help enlighten his understanding.

But the natural man does not receive the things of the Spirit of God, for they are foolishness to him; nor can he know them, because they are spiritually discerned.

1 Corinthians 2:14

Since you were not born spiritually first, there must be a rebirth in the spirit to comprehend the things of God. You were born physically first, and now you are to be born again, meaning born for the second time, spiritually. You can look in a mirror, and you will see no changes in the way you look; you will still have the same outward appearance as before. However, you are not to consider the things of old once you are born again, but walk in the newness of your life.

Therefore, if anyone is in Christ, he is a new creation; old things have passed away; behold, all things have become new.

2 Corinthians 5:17

A new creation is the rebirth of the human spirit. The real you is a spirit, you have a soul (mind, will, and emotions), and you live in a body. God deals with the *real* you, your "spirit" being, and it is the spirit that has the second birth. Left in its condition, it is capable of having the same thoughts, fears, doubts, anxiety, believing what it sees, and wrong thinking. For this reason, it needs to be renewed to think in the way God thinks. A person becomes what he or she is thinking. As Proverbs 23:7 tells us, "For as he thinks in his heart, so is he." The way of the world and its way of thinking will try to take hold and bombard your mind, and have an influence in the way you think and see things. But God's ways are higher than the world's or your ways of thinking. He did not call the things that actually were; He called those things that were not in existence as though they were. As Christians, we must read, study, meditate on, and hear the Word of God, for it is a safe place for the mind to be renewed in the way that God thinks and sees things.

As a new creature in Christ Jesus, and when first coming into the knowledge of this revelation, it was hard on my flesh to line up in the area of calling things that were not as though they were. My old way of thinking was it was telling a lie to say that I was healed when my body was sick, that I was prospering when life was a financial struggle, or that my family was saved when they were acting worldly. Thank God for the Holy Spirit coming to my rescue to help me in calling things that were not one evening when tears were flowing down my face. I heard the Holy Spirit in that moment say to me, "Say you are more than conquerors in Christ Jesus." I was in a very emotional state, and I needed to pull out of it, so I agreed with the Holy Spirit and said, "I am more than conquerors in Christ Jesus," only to hear the Holy Spirit say to me, "Say it again." So again, I said, "I am more than conquerors in Christ Jesus." Again, the Holy Spirit spoke: "Say it again." For the third time, I said, "I am more than conquerors in Christ Jesus." Know that the first time I orally gave voice to the Holy Spirit's instructions, I did not feel like a conqueror. As a matter of fact, I felt like a wimp who was already defeated. But by the third time I said those words, I felt strong. An inner healing had taken place, and I truly felt like a conqueror. My attitude changed, the tone in my voice changed, and my spirit was enlightened with the knowledge of who I am in Christ Jesus, causing the tears to dry up from my face. Everything became new, all because I chose to obey the Spirit of the Lord and got in agreement with the Holy Spirit. I had been held captive in the arena of my soul, my mind, my will, and my emotions. During the tears, I had not yet taken hold of doing what needed to be done to be set free in my mind. The mind was trapped in its way of thinking, wanting to entertain itself by means of having a pity party. My mind-set needed a fix, a change, in order to regenerate its thoughts. The spoken Word of God penetrated my heart, causing me to want a change in my thought pattern. Speaking God's Word redirected, revived, and refreshed me. The stronghold that had gripped my mind was broken, causing me to be restored. Speaking what was not so about my condition is what revived me, and also a revelation to me birthed by the Spirit of the Lord. The Holy Spirit was and is a Comforter, Teacher, and Guide in my time of distress.

> For the word of God is living and powerful, and sharper than any two-edged sword, piercing even to the division of soul and spirit, and of joints and marrow, and is a discerner of the thoughts and intents of the heart.
>
> Hebrews 4:12

The Word of God is powerful enough that anyone who chooses can be restored, healed, delivered, and set free from any attacks that try to attach themselves through the mind. It is the devil, the thief, who comes to steal, kill, and destroy with his fiery darts to control the state of mind. But there is no more need for bondage. Jesus came that you may have life and that you may have it more abundantly, and He has given you a way out of the snare of the enemy. You have a choice to come on the Lord's side by speaking the Word of God over your circumstances. Therefore, apply it in your life; it really works! The Word of God works, and when it's activated, you will see the results you really want to see. Whatever the mind can conceive, it can accomplish, whether positive or negative. Feeding the mind with the Word of God stimulates the mind to God's way of doing things. What is sown into the mind will be a person's outcome. The Word of God is a helmet of salvation meant to be your head covering. In the head is a mind in need of this helmet of God. When you are feeding your mind the Word of God, you are keeping in place this helmet of salvation to protect you from Satan's strongholds, which come through thoughts. No one has to be beat up by the strategy of the devil attacking with his fiery darts through the mind, but can instead bring his or her thoughts into the obedience of Christ.

We have a part to play here to cast down and throw away anything that is contrary to the Word of God. God has given us His only begotten Son to die for us, that we might live. He has sent His Word to heal us. He has not left us comfortless, but sent the Holy Spirit to help us. The rest is up to us to take hold of in faith. Doing our part means believing in our hearts and confessing with our mouths. With the heart, one believes unto righteousness, and with the mouth, confession is made unto salvation. Confession is a declaration or statement that you make. When you are confessing, you are saying something. Say what God's words say about you. Renewing the mind is our way of escaping and pulling down strongholds that are held captive in it. The Word of God is mighty; it is a spiritual weapon set in place to restore, heal, revive, and deliver a mind-set. The devil's confinement of control, doubt, and unbelief will be null and void once the mind is renewed.

For anything to be renewed and transformed, it must first have been damaged and in need of repair. If you want to change old habits and thoughts, study, read, and hear the Word of God. You may have to change whom you are talking with and getting advice from if they are not speaking the truth of God's Word in love to you. We need people in our lives who will stand on God's Word and not compromise it just to say what you want them to say. People who know the truth of God's Word and will speak the truth into your life so you can be set free.

As previously explained, the condition is you must abide in God's Word (John 8:31-32), (other translations say, "If you continue in My Word"), and then you are disciples indeed. Abiding or continuing in the Word of God liberates you from anything that tries to keep you in bondage. It's by abiding in the Word of God that you will "know the truth, and the truth shall make you free." If you really want to be free from wrong thoughts to obtain a better life, continue in God's Word, know the truth, and the truth will make you free.

There was a battle going on in my mind when I first came into the knowledge of abiding in God's Word, and calling those things that were not as though they were. Being an honest person, I really thought I would be lying if I did that. This was all new to me. How can this be? It's taking it by faith and believing in God's Word. One day it came to me that although I didn't see God, I believe He exists, that He and His Word are one and the same. That was a real revelation to me. One day I wrote Scriptures on three-by-five-inch index cards and placed them on the walls throughout my house. Whenever I was in one of the rooms where there were index cards, I would take time and speak the Word of God that was written on the cards. This is how I initiated getting the Word of God into my heart so whenever I needed to speak His Word over my circumstances, the Word was in my heart to speak out. The Word of God is real; it's quick and alive, and the devil does not want you to speak His Word. The enemy wants to keep you trapped in your thoughts and mind, but you are to cast down every thought and make it captive to the obedience of Christ.

> For the weapons of our warfare are not carnal but mighty in God for pulling down strongholds, casting down arguments and every high thing that exalts itself against the knowledge of God, bringing every thought into captivity to the obedience of Christ.
>
> 2 Corinthians 10:4-5

Strongholds try to take you in your thoughts, but you are to cast them down. Bring not *some* thoughts, but "every thought into captivity to the obedience of Christ." People can differentiate thoughts that are positive or negative, pure or tainted, truth or lies, clean or dirty, good or bad, lovely or ugly, right or wrong. What has to happen is you have to get rid of the negative thoughts and keep the good, positive thoughts that are of God.

> Finally, brethren, whatever things are true, whatever things are noble, whatever things are just, whatever things are pure, whatever things are lovely, whatever things are of good report, if

there is any virtue and if there is anything praise-worthy—meditate on these things.

Philippians 4:8

We all have to work daily on the thoughts that pop up in our heads. If they are contrary to God's thoughts and His way of doing things, we have to bring them into obedience to His Word. God's Word may not make sense to your natural mind; that's why your mind has to be renewed to His way of thinking.

"For My thoughts are not your thoughts, nor are your ways My ways," says the Lord. "For as the heavens are higher than the earth, so are My ways higher than your ways, and My thoughts than your thoughts."

Isaiah 55:8-9

If a bad or negative thought comes to you, it is not of God, for God is good all the time. Should you get a bad report from the doctor, you are to believe God's report, for His report says you are healed. God is more complex than we are, for we can only glimpse what He has planned for us. It is our responsibility to take Him at His Word and believe that what He says is real. Your mind did not get born again; it may want to give you a fit. However, the more you spend time in the Word of God, the more your mind will become renewed, redeveloped to see things the way God sees things. Eventually, you will change and have a different outlook on life and the things that surround you. Another good thing about having a renewed mind is that it brings freedom. You will learn not to be so quick to give in to a spirit of worry and care. Having the mind of Christ means having these attributes of love toward others, fellowship of the Spirit, mercy, and not self-seekingness.

Therefore if there is any consolation in Christ, if any comfort of love, if any fellowship of the Spirit, if any affection and mercy, fulfill my joy by being like-minded, having the same love, being of one accord, of one mind. Let nothing be done through selfish ambition or conceit, but in lowliness of mind let each esteem others better than himself. Let each of you look out not only for his own interests, but also for the interests of others.

Philippians 2:1-4

Though He, the Son of God, came in the flesh, He did not come to be served, but to serve. He went about doing good and healing all who were oppressed by the devil, for God was with Him. Jesus was not mindful of Himself, but of being about His Father's business with others in mind. Our mind-sets must be changed if we are to have the mind of Christ. The Scripture tells us in Colossians 3:2, "Set your mind on things above, not on things on the earth." How is your mind set?

If you are having a challenge in your thought life, start with reading the Bible daily. You have to put forth effort when you set to do anything. Intentionally "set" your mind as you set other things in your life. People set clocks, tables, plates, televisions, goals, and even set limits on what they will or will not do. When you set something, it's usually set on purpose; so should your mind-sets purposely be on things above. Set your thoughts to be His thoughts, change your mind from its normal way of thinking, and see things in the way in which God sees them. Search the Scriptures to see what the Word is saying about matters of life. Sometimes before you act, ask yourself, "What would Jesus do"? That thought alone will automatically keep you in line and doing right things. Practice speaking the Word of God; allow the Word sown in your heart to become real to you.

For the word of God is living and powerful, and sharper than any two-edged sword, piercing even to the division of soul and spirit, and of joints and marrow, and is a discerner of the thoughts and intents of the heart. And there is no creature hidden from His sight, but all things are naked and open to the eyes of Him to whom we must give account.

Hebrews 4:12-13

The Word of God is alive and will empower you to overcome anything in opposition of or disagreement with it.

Your mind sometimes will wander off, but you have the ability to concentrate and to bring your mind into submission to God's Word, His will, with the help of the Holy Spirit. Your old mind-set may be stuck on one way of thinking. You may think, "Nothing good ever happens to me," "I never have enough money," "No one likes me," and even, "I'm always sick." If so, instead, say, "Goodness and mercy follow me all the days of my life," "My God supplies all my needs according to His riches in glory by Christ Jesus," "I have the favor of God and man," and "By Jesus Christ's stripes I am healed." Say it! God's way sounds and is better, and your spirit will be lifted, making you feel confident and better. When you renew your mind, you will break free from the captivity of your old way of thinking and move forward to a better way of living. If you are living according to the flesh, your mind-set will be on the things of the flesh.

For those who live according to the flesh set their minds on the things of the flesh, but those who live according to the Spirit, the things of the Spirit. For to be carnally minded is death, but to be spiritually minded is life and peace. Because

the carnal mind is enmity against God; for it is not subject to the law of God, nor indeed can be.
Romans 8:5-7

We must work on not being of a carnal mind that is connected with the appetites and passions of the flesh, but have the mind-set to live according to the Spirit in order to have victory as our outcome. Examine yourself to locate where you are. Are you walking after the deeds of the flesh? Are you more concerned with natural things, such as selfish ambition, sorcery, outbursts of wrath, fame, appearances, drinking, hatred, profanity, reputation, sex, greed, and worldly gain? If you are, these are flesh deeds. Do you prefer to be spiritually minded and have life and peace? Is your life producing the fruits of the Spirit, as in Galatians 5:22-23, love, peace, kindness, goodness, long-suffering, faithfulness, gentleness, and self-control? These things are far better than the deeds of the flesh and what the world has to offer.

You will keep him in perfect peace, whose mind is stayed on You, because he trusts in You.
Isaiah 26:3

And the peace of God, which surpasses all understanding, will guard your hearts and minds through Christ Jesus.
Philippians 4:7

Make a conscious decision to renew your mind with the Word of God, and you will have life and peace when your mind is stayed on Him. Keep your attitude the same as Christ's—an attitude of pleasing the Father, "that you put off, concerning your former conduct, the old man which grows corrupt according to the deceitful lusts, and be renewed in the spirit of your mind" (Ephesians

4:22-23). He will keep those in perfect peace whose minds are stayed on Him (Isaiah 26:3). "For 'who has known the mind of the Lord that he may instruct Him?' But we have the mind of Christ" (1 Corinthians 2:16). Having the mind of Christ means having His views, plans, and way of living. "For God has not given us a spirit of fear, but of power and of love and of a sound *mind*" (2 Timothy 1:7, emphasis added).

The test: Transforming and renewing the mind.

The trial: Keeping thoughts in line with God when opposition arrives.

The testimony: Speaking the Word of God, good thoughts, a sound mind, and walking in perfect peace.

Pray this prayer: *Father, You and Your Word are one and the same. I will guard my heart and thoughts to line up with Your Word. I will put Your Word in remembrance. Thank You for giving me Your Holy Spirit as my Helper to bring all your words to my remembrance. I purpose to trust You with all my heart and lean not on my own understanding, my own thoughts, for Your thoughts and Your ways are higher than my thoughts and my ways. Whenever things look as if they are not working and the devil tries to offer me doubt in my mind, I will cast down any stronghold and bring my thoughts into obedience to Christ Jesus. Father, You have given me Your Spirit, and I choose to be spiritually minded and not carnal-minded. Thank You that I have peace, because my mind is stayed on You. In Jesus' name I pray. Amen.*

Be anxious for nothing, but in everything by
prayer and supplication, with thanksgiving,
let your request be made known to God;
and the peace of God,
which surpasses all understanding,
will guard your hearts and minds
through Christ Jesus.
Philippians 4:6-7

Abiding in the Place of Safety

He who dwells in the secret place of the Most High
shall abide under the shadow of the Almighty.

Psalm 91:1

Who is the "he" in this verse? I believe that this
"he" is a collective noun that refers to a widespread people of commonality. This "he" does not pertain only to the masculine gender. The word "he" in this
text refers to any person, male or female.

When you have made the Lord God your abiding
place, nothing can overtake you because there is nothing
bigger or greater than God. Everything you need is in
the secret place of the Most High—your safe haven, a
place of protection, your deliverance, your healing, your
provision, and His love. As we read Psalm 91, we can
see there are many blessings and benefits to dwelling in
the secret place of the Most High:

- "He shall deliver you from the snare of the fowler
  and from the perilous pestilence" (v. 3).
- "He shall cover you with His feathers" (v. 4).
- "And under His wings you shall take refuge" (v. 4).
- "His truth shall be your shield and buckler" (v. 4).
- "You shall not be afraid of the terror by night" (v. 5).
- "Nor of the arrow that flies by day" (v. 5).
- "Nor of the pestilence that walks in darkness" (v. 6).

- "Nor of the destruction that lays waste at noonday" (v. 6).
- "A thousand may fall at your side, and ten thousand at your right hand; but it shall not come near you" (v. 7). Although things surround you in this world's economy, you do not have to be moved; they will not come close to you.
- "Only with your eyes shall you look, and see the reward of the wicked" (v. 8). This is your victory over the devil, who has tried to take you out.
- "No evil shall befall you" (v. 10). Hallelujah! This will not occur and emerge.
- "Nor shall any plague come near your dwelling" (v. 10).
- "He shall give His angels charge over you, to keep you in all your ways" (v. 11).
- "In their hands they shall bear you up, lest you dash your foot against a stone" (v. 12).
- "You shall tread upon the lion and the cobra" (v. 13).
- "The young lion and the serpent you shall trample underfoot" (v. 13).
- He will deliver you (v. 14).
- You will be set on high because you know His name (v. 14).
- You shall call upon Him, and He will answer you (v. 15).
- He will be with you in trouble; He will deliver and honor you (v. 15).
- With long life He will satisfy you and show His salvation (v. 16).

The first blessing mentioned in this chapter is that we will be delivered from the fowler, someone who hunts, catches, or traps. This, without doubt, would be our adversary, the devil, as well as the "perilous pestilence," which can be a virus or deadly disease. God has given us the answer to anything that may rise up against us, a place to run to for safety, the secret place of the Most High. When you dwell in the secret place, the devil can't touch you (1 John 5:18). He cannot enter this secret place where God dwells. God is our Protection twenty-four hours a day from fear, terror, sickness, and disease. He is our Deliverer, our Safeguard. In Him we can trust, resting assured that there's total security and no harm or evil shall come close to us. We do not have to be afraid. Imagine having a shelter so safe and secure that nothing could harm or even touch you in any negative way. Who would not want that? Run to Him, for He is everything that you will need! Don't go in the opposite direction of Him; He is a Friend who will stick closer than any. He is the Answer.

You truly have a safe haven when you have someone who loves you so much, someone who allows you to put your guard down to where you may have relaxation and rest from all your cares, someone whom you can totally trust. You may ask, "How can I have this safe place? Is there truly such a place, and does it cost me anything?" The price has already been paid. You only have to receive Jesus Christ as your Lord and Savior, and take up residence, dwelling in God. Jesus Christ is the revelation of God's salvation for whosoever will come. Yet, there are so many people who spend so much of their energy and time on other things, such as the workplace, the television, other entertainment, or sports, and they fail to give more, or even equal, time to entering into the presence of God through praying, reading the Bible, going to church, and worshiping and praising Him. Why is it that the Creator of heaven and earth, the One who has made the world and everything good in it, is put on the back burner in the lives of so many? He is the Giver of life, and without Him, we would not exist; we would not be able to live or move without Him.

For in Him we live and move and have our being, as also some of your own poets have said, "For we are also His offspring."

Acts 17:28

We are His offspring, His children, and we have a right to dwell in Him. It should be as common for us as it is for biological children to dwell in their parents' home. Even though children eventually leave the home in which they grew up, they will feel quite comfortable about coming back to the place where they once lived because it's familiar ground. Most children always go back to their home. God, your heavenly Father, is your Home in which to abide, your Refuge, a Place of shelter, the Place that you make your abode. The physical place where we live shelters us from everything that's outside of it. It protects us from storms, rain, thieves, and cares of the world. It's a place where you are able to be yourself and settle down. God's place is a spiritual place in which to dwell where anyone can have all that is offered in Psalm 91. You cannot get to this dwelling place by car, airplane, train, bus, telephone, or e-mail. So how do you get there? It will take some of your time. You must seek Him with all your heart, soul, and mind. God is a spirit, and they that worship Him must worship Him in spirit and in truth.

But the hour is coming, and now is, when the true worshipers will worship the Father in spirit and truth; for the Father is seeking such to worship Him. God is Spirit, and those who worship Him must worship in spirit and truth.

John 4:23-24

When you are a true worshiper, you love God, giving Him adoration, reverence, and respect. Imagine that! The thought that God actually seeks those who will do that for Him tells us that He desires to have worship. Will you love Him? Will you adore Him? Will you devote time to Him? Will you do this not only in spirit, but also in truth? God wants the real deal, the heart that will worship Him. Trying to fake it will not make it; counterfeits won't do. God cannot be fooled. He sees the heart and knows the genuine. Besides, doesn't He deserve the best and nothing less? You would expect the same in return, wouldn't you? Enter His gates with thanksgiving and His courts with praise; love and adore Him. Prayer is an immense vehicle for spending time with Him. Talk to God sincerely, with a pure heart. He wants you to come to Him. It demonstrates reverence when you acknowledge Him; it shows you believe He exists and that He is the Answer.

A lot of people want a quick fix and expect God to be Johnny-on-the-spot when there's an emergency in their lives. Why should anyone expect Him to be part of his or her life when the person has shut Him out? He can't be part of your life, at least not in the way you desire, if you are not willing to take time and abide in Him. It's your choice to dwell or not to dwell, to abide or not to abide. The choice is each individual's to make. Whom will you serve? Choose this day to serve the Lord. All are welcome to come have His shelter, for it is not His will that anyone is apart from His safety. God is no respecter of persons.

For "whoever calls on the name of the Lord shall be saved."

Romans 10:13

Everyone has tests, trials, and temptations that arise in their lives. What needs to be remembered is there is a place of safety you can abide in. God is our Refuge and Strength, a very present Help in trouble. He is a right-now God. He is there and will always be there for those who are dwelling in Him. He will never leave or forsake you, for He is faithful. When all else has failed you, look to God, who never fails. He is the Alpha and the Omega, the Beginning and the End. He is there when things are looking good, calm, and triumphant, and He is there in the darkness of the midnight hour, when all seems to come crashing down on you. God is always there. Run to this place of safety, the Lord God, your Dwelling Place. He is your Deliverance.

One day the Lord was dealing with my heart, telling me to spend some time with Him prostrate, lying flat on my face every day. Each morning as I awoke, I got up and lay on the floor. Sometimes I prayed and I praised, and sometimes I was quiet, waiting in His presence for Him. During the weeks of spending daily time dwelling in Him, there was a work taking place. My heart, my priorities, my life was being altered. Cares were rolled over onto the Lord. Change was taking place. I knew my time spent in His presence was bringing about change. I couldn't be touched by anything or anybody. Nothing could penetrate the bond, this union we had, for I was in a safe place. I didn't care what was going on around me, or what should have been going on. I was not concerned with things around me, for I was in Him, and He in me, and nothing else mattered. Each time I arose from the floor, being in His presence, there was a protection, an anointing that covered me. I was walking in His truth, shielded and buckled close to Him. The fiery darts may have come sometime afterward, but they could not pierce me, for I was guarded in His protection

You must make a conscious decision to come and dwell in the secret place of the Most High. It's soothing, peaceful, calm, restful, and comforting. Try dwelling with Him; I promise you will love it. You will have to make time for Him. Make Him your first priority in your life. Living apart from God is a spiritual death sentence, but when He is first in your life, everything else will fall into place.

> But seek first the kingdom of God and His righteousness, and all these things shall be added to you.
>
> Matthew 6:33

I used to hear this Scripture quoted a lot in my former church, and wondered what the kingdom of God was. I did not understand what the kingdom of God was, and I wanted to seek it out. I decided to search the Scriptures to enlighten my understanding, and found this verse concerning the kingdom of God:

> For the kingdom of God is not eating and drinking, but righteousness and peace and joy in the Holy Spirit.
>
> Romans 14:17

When one is seeking the kingdom of God, he or she is seeking God's way of doing things by means of three key things: righteousness, peace, and joy in the Holy Spirit. Therefore, if you are seeking righteousness, peace, and joy in the Holy Spirit, you are seeking the kingdom of God. His kingdom does not and will not have unrighteousness, disharmony, disagreement, war, fighting, sadness, worry, or unhappiness.

We were made the righteousness of God through Christ Jesus (2 Corinthians 5:21). It is right living that demonstrates the product of righteousness. When you know you are the righteousness of Christ Jesus, there is a boldness and confidence in the things that are in right standing. You may not always feel like doing what's right, but doing right fits into the package of righteousness. Once you are a new creature in Christ Jesus, you can most definitely distinguish right versus wrong. Righteousness is always with you. It is who you are, whether or not you choose to obey and do right. It is your safe place, given to you in which to abide.

There were several times when I got on my knees to have peace restored in relationships with people in the body of Christ. I would think, *My God, why do I do these things? People will think I'm a pushover.* I remembered the Word of God concerning seeking peace, to pursue peace with all men, and how peace is to be the umpire of our hearts. It takes God and a person with a willing heart to make the change to do the things that are pleasing in His sight and to glorify Him. In the kingdom of God, there is peace, for He is a God of peace.

There was a time when every year during the Christmas season, I would become sad. I knew that Jesus was the reason for the season. But I allowed all the festivity and joy during this time of year displayed through the commercials, malls, and store displays, along with Christmas music filling the atmosphere, decorations, and the happiness of Christmas and families coming together to somewhat put a strain on my having joy. You see, after the children in my family grew up and left home, we didn't come together for this holiday season, so there was no joy there. I felt lonely and sad. Then one day I heard the Spirit of the Lord say to me, "Stop having a pity party, and you make a difference." Many people did not have family, friends, or a place to go this time of year, and I could invite some over to celebrate with us the joy of the Christmas season. I was pregnant with my first child when I stepped out in faith on this and invited some people over. The joy filled our hearts, and a change took place. I now say, "God gave me Christmas." For more than twenty-seven years, we have celebrated Christmas in our home, and to this day, Christmas is my favorite holiday to celebrate with family and friends. Jesus Christ was all the time, and still is, the reason for the Christmas season. I wanted to celebrate Jesus by coming together with others, and God's love reached out to me, told me what to do, and has made a radical change in my life, giving me the desires of my heart. He is a good God. He restored my soul by giving me joy and peace in the place of sadness.

To seek His kingdom is to seek that which is good spiritually, and not that which is based on foods or material things, or what we may or may not see. "The kingdom of God does not come with observation; nor will they say, 'See here!' or 'See there!' For indeed, the kingdom of God is within you" (Luke 17:20-21). God is good all the time, and His kingdom is a happy, right-standing place, which dwells within you to show forth God's glory. If it's not right, you are not to have a part in it. If it's not in peace, move from it, and if it's something that's robbing you of joy, flee from it. God's kingdom is governed by Him; it's a kingdom of righteous living, with unity of love, peace, tranquility, and harmony. His place is a fortress that will remain. All uncleanness dwells outside of it. No evil shall dwell there. Take a break from the hiccups of life, enter into God's place of residence, and be seated with peace of mind in all that may concern you. If you have a need to abide in a place of safety, go to God! *Abide* in His Word, for He and His Word are one and the same (John 1:1). In John 15:7, Jesus says, "If you abide in Me, and My words abide in you, you will ask what you desire, and it shall be done for you." Keep His commandments, and you will "abide" in His love (John 15:10). He is your Refuge, your safe Haven, your "abiding" Place, and in Him you will find rest.

The test: To dwell or not to dwell in the secret place of the Most High.

The trial: Weighing your priorities.

The testimony: Dwelling in the secret place of the Most High, we have God's protection, a new place of residence.

Pray this prayer: *Father, I thank You for providing a place in You where I may come dwell. You are my Protector, my Shield, and my Buckler. If I seem to be drawing away from You, Father, tug at my heart to get my attention, that I may come again and make my abode with You. I ask You, Father, to put me in check, should I stumble by making the cares of life a priority over You. In that I do repent, for You are my Refuge and my Fortress, and in You I will put my trust. You will never leave me or forsake me. I thank You, Father, for being my safe Haven. You are the one true God, and besides You, there is no other. As I seek Your kingdom first and Your righteousness, I thank You that all things good shall be added to me. Father, thank You that I do not have to be afraid of any attacks from the enemy because I have made You my Habitation. You are my Deliverer, and You will honor me. And Father, I thank You that You satisfy me with long life and show me Your salvation. It is my desire to please You. In You, I will make a conscious decision to dwell in the secret place of the Most High, and I shall abide under the shadow of You, God, the Almighty. In Jesus' name I pray. Amen.*

Tell it

To everything there is a season, a time for every purpose under heaven. . . . A time to tear, and a time to sew; a time to keep silence, and a time to speak.

Ecclesiastes 3:1, 7

The words "tell it" came to me by the Spirit of the Lord some years ago for a chapter in this book. Of course, I responded, "Tell what?" "Tell it"—how the Lord has delivered you from sickness and how God's grace has set the captive free from the snare of the enemy. "Tell it"— His goodness, His mercy, and His kindness. "Tell it"—how the devil has tried to take your life several times. "Tell it"—how God has kept you and is able to keep others from being tricked, misled, even from being deceived. And "tell it"—how God would show you things to come by His Spirit.

"Tell it" jubilantly echoed within my spirit, as if bouncing, dancing bubbles were celebrating with a sort of enthusiasm, waiting to be heard in the hope of giving help and hope, and setting others free. But the questions in my soul penetrated with reluctance: *Why would anyone want to know this about me, and furthermore, who cares? Who am I?* These thoughts occupied my mind, yet the words of the Lord illuminated my spirit to recognize His words clearly. "Tell it" does tell chronicles about me; conversely, it is for God to be glorified. I felt I should just do it, "tell it," allowing God to be God, and doubt not.

With that being said, I will start by telling how, when I was five years old, the Lord delivered me from a sporadically occurring condition of epilepsy, a chronic disorder of the nervous system characterized by a partial or complete loss of consciousness and sometimes convulsions. With me it was the loss of consciousness; I had blackouts because of a disturbance in the normal electrical rhythm of brain cells. At approximately age five is my first memory of having an episode of epilepsy. After being carried in my dad's arms, when I was about to be placed inside a vehicle to be taken to the hospital, I became conscious enough to see that this vehicle was a hearse. My dad drove for a funeral home during this time, and it so happened he had the hearse at our home on this day.

Upon approaching the hearse and with a little awareness that I was about to be placed inside it, I suddenly blurted out, "I don't want to ride in there." That's all I can recall because I lost consciousness. As a teenager, my mother told me she had taken me, at the young age of five, to a Pentecostal church for the pastor to pray for me concerning the epilepsy. She also informed me that after the pastor had prayed for me, there were no more epileptic episodes, that God had healed me. Praise God for His mighty working healing power, and my mother for coming to the knowledge of the truth of His Word concerning healing.

And these signs will follow those who believe: In My name they will cast out demons; they will speak with new tongues; they will take up serpents; and if they drink anything deadly, it will by no means hurt them; they will lay hands on the sick, and they will recover.

Mark 16:17-18

My mother had read from the Bible the above text: "they will lay hands on the sick, and they will recover." Wanting healing for me, her daughter, she asked her then pastor about this Scripture she had read, only to be told that healing was done away with. You see, the church my mother had been attending did not believe healing was for us today, causing her to wonder, *Why not?* After all, she had seen and read it in the Bible. So she searched for another church that believed in the above text. Visiting a Pentecostal Holy Ghost-filled church, my mother asked the pastor there about this Scripture, which he believed was still for us today. The pastor in faith laid hands on me, praying for me in Jesus' name to be healed. After hands were laid on me to be healed of the epilepsy, I never had another episode. Praise God!

Witnessing God's hand of deliverance in my life through the power of prayer and the laying on of hands caused my mother to leave the church she had been attending and join the Pentecostal church, which believes in miracles, signs, and wonders for the church today. She said she read it in the Bible for herself and thought it strange that the church she had been attending did not believe in what was written in the Bible. So it was there in the Pentecostal church that I grew and learned to know Jesus Christ as my Lord and Savior. God still is in the healing business, for He is the same yesterday, today and forever. God has not retired from healing. He wants His children to be free from all sickness and disease. If your natural father or mother wants you free from sickness and disease, wouldn't you think your heavenly Father would want the same for you? God does not want His children to be broken, sick, and diseased; He is a good God and wants nothing but good for you. Believe and receive what rightfully belongs to you as a child of God.

While I grew up with five siblings, God's hand was upon my life. When I was a child in sixth grade, around eleven years of age, the Lord had me speak of some things that were going to take place concerning all the children in our household, including myself, by the time we finished school. Who was going to believe an eleven-year-old child saying something that was to come years ahead? Neither they, nor I could see what was being said in the natural world, and therefore, they did not believe me. I was told I was making things up, but there was a deep knowing inside me that was as real to me as my knowing my name. I knew what was spoken was true. I could not explain it at that time; however, a revelation of truth was moving greatly within me, like an avalanche rolling down a mountainside, not to be denied, but to be *told*. If you had asked me at that very moment how I knew these things, or where I was getting this information, I almost certainly would have answered simply, "I just know it." When you absolutely know something, no one can take that truth away from you. Without a doubt, you will take a stand firmly on what you know. No one can persuade you that your name is anything other than what you have been called all your life. It's on your birth certificate, your license, and your bills; you know that you know your name. This knowing was deep within me, as surely as I knew my name. I never hesitated, nor did I question, myself as to why these things were being said. I just knew. There was no pressure or force, but an assurance to suddenly say what I knew in my heart with ease. Then I would go on about my chores or whatever I had been doing as a child. As the school years progressed, every word happened to come to pass exactly as I had spoken it at the tender age of eleven. The Lord brought back to my remembrance all I had spoken years earlier as each event occurred. Did this come upon me after hands were laid on me in prayer by the Pentecostal preacher, or as I was sitting under the power of the Holy Spirit in the church ser-vices? I did not receive the baptism of the Holy Spirit until a year later, at age twelve. What I do know is that as a child, I wanted God, I wanted everything that He was, for He was then and is still good, and I wanted to have good in my life. Only the Lord Himself knows when He touched and appointed me with this knowledge.

In addition, as a teenager between the age of fifteen and sixteen, I told my mother something when she and I were alone in the kitchen, and subsequently, I was told to stop lying. *Lying?* I would think. *I am not lying.* Why would I lie? I have always had an extreme aver-sion to anyone's lying. As a matter of fact, if I am aware that anyone habitually lies, I honestly do not care to talk with that person for the very reason that he or she is going to lie. Why listen? Who wants to be told lies? I don't—do you? One of six things God hates is "a lying tongue" (Proverbs 6:17). Most definitely, lying is not my forte. I don't like it, and I do not want to have anything to do with it. I don't care to be around anyone who lies, for it is the opposite of who God is and should not be part of any of His children's characters.

Bear in mind that there were three things in par-ticular that were told to my mother at different times, the *first* concerning each of my siblings, the changes that would occur with each of them during their high school years. One was drafted into the Army immedi-ately after high school, one went to Job Corps, and the others took total detours in different directions, like what was told her. When I told her this, she thought it was very funny and started to laugh. *Second*, I told my mom to be watchful driving, for I saw her car in an accident in which the car was totaled. She responded, "Tricia (the name family and friends called me), stop lying," and she looked at me and shook her head. A few weeks later, there was an accident in which her car was totaled, but thanks to God, she came out of the accident without a scratch. *Third*, I told her to take my sister to the doctor, for she was pregnant. At the time I said it, my sister was in the beginning stage, possibly a month pregnant. My sister did not have knowledge herself that she was carrying a child. Neither did I before this sudden insight came to me. I remember that I was wiping the dining room table as I told my mom. There had been no thoughts about my sister, no plans to say this or to make something up just to be talking. It was an immediate revelation on the inside of me that came out to be known and told. There had to be some concern later about these words I had spoken, because a few weeks later, Mom did take my sister to the doctor, and found out she was indeed pregnant. I was a young teenage child who was somewhat sheltered from the world outside; I literally did not go anywhere other than church and school, and I was occasionally allowed to play in the front yard. I felt like the black sheep and the behind-the-scenes child in the family, yet God used me through spoken words that were not observable to the natural eyes. I can remember each occurrence clearly to this day, how God reminded me of each as it came to pass. You should never underestimate God's working through and using children, for He uses those whom He chooses. If you are a parent, don't disregard it should your child happen to speak something to you that is not evident to your eyes. He or she may be speaking by the Spirit of the Lord. There is such an innocence and humbleness within children, and Jesus advised us to be converted and become as little children. Jesus used a little child as an example to speak to the disciples who were concerned with who is the greatest in the kingdom of heaven.

> Then Jesus called a little child to Him, set him in the midst of them, and said, "Assuredly, I say to you, unless you are converted and become as little

children, you will by no means enter the kingdom of heaven. Therefore whoever humbles himself as this little child is the greatest in the kingdom of heaven. Whoever receives one little child like this in My name receives Me."

Matthew 18:2-5

What was the "like this" in the little child that Jesus was speaking of? It was the child's humility that He spoke of in verse 4. We know there are also children who are not so humble, so Jesus used a child who had humility. Jesus is saying to be converted and become humble as the little child He put before them. Children are a heritage given to you by God and should not be underestimated or taken too lightly. Parents, you are responsible for the training of your children in the ways of the Lord. Be especially aware how you treat children, for you will be held accountable.

I have a tendency to think, when I hear of adults behaving with appalling conduct, *What happened to them when they were children?* You see, in life everyone will have choices to make that will decide his or her fate. You can have several children in the same home environment, and there may be one who will carry on with the habits that surrounded them, and one who will do the opposite. Let's say there were children in a household where there was lots of drinking of alcoholic beverages. One child may grow up thinking it's okay and pick up the habit. Another child, witnessing the same, chooses never to touch alcohol because of seeing what it did to his or her family. Although life is about making right and wrong choices, as parents we should live a good example for our children. "Train up a child in the way he should go, and when he is old he will not depart from it" (Proverbs 22:6). Ask yourself how your child is being trained and whether that is the way from which you would not want them to depart. If you previously have not been a good example for them, it's not too late to change, pray for your children, and thank God for His loving-kindness and tender mercies. Children are a heritage from the Lord. The Bible states: "Don't you see that children are God's best gift" Psalm 127:3 (Message)? What someone does with the gift of children given to him or her by God will show whether or not the person appreciates that gift. Some people cherish and take pride in their gift; some put their gift up and ignore it. Some abuse and even give their gift away. Be one who appreciates and treasures the gift given to them by God. Don't be confused about who children are. They are your gift! Don't be a source of affliction to your children; they are a product of their environment. God is able to deliver anyone from a life that is headed for destruction. Call on the name of the Lord to be saved, delivered, and set free.

> Call to Me, and I will answer you, and show you great and mighty things, which you do not know.
> Jeremiah 33:3

> And it shall come to pass that whoever calls on the name of the Lord shall be saved. For in Mount Zion and in Jerusalem there shall be deliverance, as the Lord has said, among the remnant whom the Lord calls.
> Joel 2:32

> For there is no distinction between Jew and Greek, for the same Lord over all is rich to all who call upon Him. For "whoever calls on the name of the Lord shall be saved."
> Romans 10:12-13

Should you ever believe you are in a place of despair, misery, depression, and gloom, or in a dark place, call on the name of the Lord, for He will hear your cry and deliver you from what is trying to destroy you. For the Lord God is your Refuge and Strength, a very present Help in trouble, and for this reason, you can always call on Him. The word "refuge" implies a shelter or protection from danger or trouble; it is a place of safety and security. I will tell you that no one can love you like God can, for He will be there whenever you need Him to be. He's a keepsake. It is the devil that comes with hate toward you with the intention of destroying your life. It is never God's fault when bad things happen, for He is the One who protects you from the intended destruction. Let me share how He has kept me from destruction, starting at a tender young age.

Several adults, including some who witness and are very reliable, have informed me that I was intentionally sat in an ant bed at the tender age of two. Why? Apparently, because I was not yet walking. The adult responsible told me that placing me in an ant bed would help me get up and walk. At around age seventeen or eighteen, a gun was put to my head, and God intervened, causing the gun not to be fired. When I was nineteen years old, I was kidnapped, beaten, drugged, raped, and taken to another state. I was threatened with being thrown in the Hudson River, a 315-mile river that flows from north to south through eastern New York. I cried out to God, praying and asking Him to help me. He heard my cry, and made a way that allowed me to escape during a time when I was not being watched. I got to a phone booth and called my parents to let them know my location, but did not reveal my situation. Then I asked a stranger for help. This person gave me money and took me to a bus station, where I had to wait hours before the scheduled bus was to depart. Every time someone opened the door to come into the bus station, I quickly went to the bathroom and hid in the stall area because I was afraid the kidnapper would come looking for me. Eventually, in came a person who took notice of my behavior and reached out and conversed with me. Of course, at first, I was skeptical, but he was very kind and sincere, and helped keep watch over me until I got on the bus. God sent me help during a time that seemed like eternity before I left to get home safely. These life occurrences reminded me of the different times the devil used people to do his evil works, and how he attempted to destroy Jesus early on in His life, when He was a young child, and also as an adult. Jesus came with a purpose. His life was not taken. He willingly "gave" His life. Although there were attempts to destroy Him, it was not yet His time.

When the angel of the Lord appeared to Joseph in a dream, he said, "Arise, take the young Child and His mother, flee to Egypt, and stay there until I bring you word; for Herod will seek the young Child to destroy Him" (Matthew 2:13). Again, when Jesus "overturned the tables of the money changers and the seats of those who sold doves, . . . the scribes and chief priests heard it and sought how they might destroy Him" (Mark 11:15, 18). Again, in Mark 12:12, "they sought to lay hands on Him, but feared the multitude." Even after Jesus had been ministering, they plotted to kill Him.

> After two days it was the Passover and the Feast of Unleavened Bread. And the chief priests and the scribes sought how they might take Him by trickery and put Him to death.
>
> Mark 14:1

You see, Jesus can identify with our afflictions; He came so that we might have life more abundantly. It is the devil's job to steal, to kill, and to destroy, if you allow him. If the devil tried from Jesus' early years to destroy Him, it's no surprise that the devil is up to his same tricks to take out God's precious gift of children starting at a young age, too. God has been merciful to me, and has been my Protection and my Healer. He raised me from a sickness meant to kill me. When I think of the goodness of the Lord and all that He has done for me, I praise God for saving and delivering me from the enemy's traps. With long life, He satisfies me and shows me His salvation.

During my early life trials, I always had a consciousness of God, for I wanted to believe in someone who was good and who would really love me. Going to church as a child gave me hope and such a hunger for God who so loved the world that He gave His only begotten son. *Wow,* I thought, *a God who saves, delivers, and sets the captives free, and a God who is love.* Oh, how I reached out for Him to just touch me with His goodness and loving-kindness, to reassure and console me with His love. I remember wanting to believe in someone as good as God in saving people. As a child, my mom told me once that she was going to whip me. I prayed and literally cried out to God, saying, "If there is a God, and you are real, please don't let my mom whip me." That was the first prayer that I remember God answering for me. My mother, who always stood by her word and carried out what she said she would do, did not whip me when it came to this incident. I wondered if she heard me crying out, praying to God, causing her to have compassion, and so she spared me. Even so, it was God who intervened and who had answered my cry. Let God be glorified for all He has done in my life, for He has shown Himself mighty time after time through His love and protection, for He has been and is a Refuge, a Place of safety.

During my Christian walk with the Lord as an adult, God also has kept me from being misled by following my emotions when it came to where He wanted me to be in a church community. When God first dealt with me by His Spirit, along with the written Word of God, and

I learned there was so much more to Him than what I had been taught, it was a bit challenging because of the bondage I was in. The church that I grew up in was very religious when it came to what you wore, how you were baptized, and its belief that the only way for someone to be saved was through the evidence of speaking in tongues. They were not ones to believe that by confessing with your mouth the Lord Jesus and believing in your heart that God has raised Christ from the dead, you will be saved (Romans 10:9). Although this verse of Scripture had been mocked, I, like my mother, knew what was written in the Bible, and I believed it. I no longer could accept the teaching that if a person did not speak in tongues, he or she was not saved. Let's look at the two-part faith of believing and receiving salvation according to the Scripture:

> But what does it say? "The word is near you, in your mouth and in your heart" (that is, the word of faith which we preach): that if you confess with your mouth the Lord Jesus and believe in your heart that God has raised Him from the dead, you will be saved.
>
> Romans 10:8-9

This text shows that two things have to happen to be saved: You must confess with your mouth the Lord Jesus, and you must believe in your heart that God has raised Him from the dead. One is in your mouth; the other, in your heart—a two-part faith. Nowhere in this Scripture passage does it say you will be saved by speaking in tongues. Let's look at several verses in Acts:

> When the Day of Pentecost had fully come, they were all with one accord in one place. And suddenly there came a sound from heaven, as of a rushing mighty wind, and it filled the whole house

where they were sitting. Then there appeared to them divided tongues, as of fire, and one sat upon each of them. And they were all filled with the Holy Spirit and began to speak with other tongues, as the Spirit gave them utterance.

Acts 2:1-4

While Peter was still speaking these words, the Holy Spirit fell upon all those who heard the word. And those of the circumcision who believed were astonished, as many as came with Peter, because the gift of the Holy Spirit had been poured out on the Gentiles also.

Acts 10:44-45

And when Paul had laid hands on them, the Holy Spirit came upon them, and they spoke with tongues and prophesied.

Acts 19:6

But you shall receive power when the Holy Spirit has come upon you; and you shall be witnesses to Me in Jerusalem, and in all Judea and Samaria, and to the end of the earth.

Acts 1:8

Romans 10:8-9 and verses in the book of Acts are speaking of two totally different things. It's like having cake and pie. They both are sweet desserts, but different. So are salvation and the Holy Spirit two different identities. Salvation is your escape to safety; it is your deliverance, your healing. Salvation rescues you from walking in darkness and takes you to walking in the kingdom and light of the Lord. When a person receives Jesus Christ as his or her Lord and Savior, His Spirit comes and dwells "within" that person. Speaking in tongues, the Holy Spirit comes "upon" you, equipping you with power for here on this earth. Going to the Word of God for myself and studying, I found out there's more to God. Having established a relationship with God through His Word and being acquainted with being led by the Holy Spirit has kept me many times from being misled. We do not have to be deceived or misled by man's misinterpretation of the Scriptures, Scriptures taken out of context, or false doctrines. God will reveal Himself to you when you seek Him for yourself diligently. It was through my searching and studying the Scriptures that the Holy Spirit dealt with my heart concerning change in my church affiliation. Reading the Bible one night, Romans 14:1-23 in its entirety, I had a conversation with God. I said to Him, "God, that is not what we are taught," and then I heard the Lord say, "What does my Word say?" Responding, I said, "Yes, I see what's written, but that's not how we are taught." Again, I heard, "What does my Word say?" Because I believed the teachings that were taught at my local assembly, I, for the third time, said, "God, this is not how we are taught," and for the third time, the Lord said, "What does my Word say?" Finally, I heard the Spirit of the Lord saying to me, "Whom are you going to believe, God or man?" I closed the Bible and said, "You, Lord." Awareness of the law of liberty and the law of love was revelation to me that night. Days after this, I had a dream of being on a ship with other Christians, and the ship sank. The dream was animated, of course, in that we were still able to breathe and stay alive under the water. All the Christians were trapped behind bars in captivity. I was standing, with my hands holding on to the bars. Suddenly, in silhouette form, a person came without flesh and grabbed my arms to pull me out to safety. I was rescued, but for some reason, I lost an arm. I did not understand, if this was an angel of the Lord who had come to rescue me, why did I lose an arm? My thinking was that an arm should not have been lost. After this dream, the Lord started dealing with me to visit a particular church the next Sunday morning. The Lord truly ordered my steps to confirm that about which He was dealing with me. I have never gotten to visit this church again on a Sunday morning. In that church service, the pastor ministered from this Scripture text:

If your right eye causes you to sin, pluck it out and cast it from you; for it is more profitable for you that one of your members perish, than for your whole body to be cast into hell. And if your right hand causes you to sin, cut it off and cast it from you; for it is more profitable for you that one of your members perish, than for your whole body to be cast into hell.

Matthew 5:29-30

This pastor explained that these two Scripture verses were not indicating that you should literally pluck out or cut off your physical members, but cut off spiritual members that might be causing you to sin. Now, during this time, I had gotten in a place of murmuring and complaining, not being happy with all the religious beliefs that were proclaimed at my local assembly. God was not happy with my murmuring and complaining. Then, one day I was saying to Him that I did not want my children growing up in all of this. I heard, "Then why are you there?" If it was not good for my children and in my sight, then it was not good for me either. Wow, that made sense to me! So I had to cut loose fellowshiping in a congregation with which I was not in total agreement. "Can two walk together, unless they are agreed?" (Amos 3:3). After this clarity, I wrote a letter to my pastor requesting that my name be taken off their membership role book. (It was a tradition that if you were on their role book, you were considered a member there.) Once I did that, I just stayed home watching Christian television with the belief that I did not need the saints. All I needed was Jesus, and I knew I had Him and I could make it with Him alone.

After several months passed, I started to long to fellowship with the saints again and would get dressed for church intending to visit and attend a particular church service. During this time, I really did not understand being led by the Holy Spirit, and as I would leave the house and start traveling toward this church, I found myself being impressed to go visit another church. I made several attempts to visit a particular church that I wanted very much to visit, but I seemingly could not make it there. To this day, I have never attended that particular church's services. I believe my steps were ordered by the Lord, and that is not where He wanted me to be. Had I gone, I might have gotten ensnared by more religious beliefs. Some time later, someone told me about the church that I currently attend. After I visited a few times, the Lord said to me, "Home," and I knew God was placing me there. After more than twenty years of membership with much growing, living, and walking my Christian walk and looking at people, I started wanting to leave. But God! The Holy Spirit arrested me. I heard, "Be still, and know that I am God" (Psalm 46:10, NIV). After I heard the Spirit of the Lord saying this to me, my nephew came to bring me a belated birthday gift. In the gift bag, he had a glass plaque with the words "Be still, and know that I am God" Psalm 46:10. My spirit leaped when I read the inscription, for it was the same, confirming what the Lord had spoken to me, and my nephew had no knowledge of it. This was God speaking, and also leading and directing me.

I truly believe God was keeping me, even from me. Father knows best, and God will help us every time to not make a wrong move. The question is, Will we override the leading and promptings of the Lord? God has placed me where He would have me to be. He knows what's ahead that may trip us up in life, for His ways are higher than our ways. When a person settles in his or her heart that God has placed the person in a particular church community, that person should come alongside that ministry in assisting it to be all that God will have it to be. Don't kick against the will of the Lord for you, but humbly submit yourself to Him. Know that it is always for the good to be led by the Spirit of the Lord, and not led by our emotions or feelings. No one has to be going from church to church when you with confidence know that God has placed you where He wants you. God does not make mistakes; it is an individual's will to override the Spirit of the Lord's leading and promptings that leads to mistakes. It also could be that instead of patiently waiting for the Spirit of the Lord to lead, one becomes anxious and consequently led by what the person may be feeling in his or her soul, which is the mind, will, and emotions. If you absolutely don't know that you have heard from God, then don't go; don't make a decision that you may later have to deal with humiliation over and then retreat from. There may be times in your life when you feel you don't belong, that you are not being used in the place of ministry that's working in your heart. You may even feel like a misfit, but wait, I say, on the Lord before making a mistake by moving too soon. Be still, and know that He is God. We are not to be led or moved by our feelings, for feelings are subject to change, nor are we to be ignorant of Satan's devices.

You may be planning on going on vacation next year, and before the vacation time arrives, you may have had several different feelings about it, causing you to make changes. Feelings are fickle and not to be relied on always. Being sensitive to and knowing the leading of the Holy Spirit, we don't have to miss it. We don't have to be tricked or even make a mistake that may cause regret. I strongly recommend praying when you want to make a move due to what you are feeling. If you are not sure if it is you or the Holy Spirit that is leading you, think about this traffic light analogy: the red light, yellow light, and green light. It's interesting that the first signal is red, indicating to come to a complete **"stop."** Don't go and quickly react because of what you may be thinking or feeling. Moving too hastily, without first examining what is really going on within you, can possibly be a big mistake. You know if you have an attitude, are upset, angry, bitter, resentful, or have other issues. You know what's working in your heart. Don't hide from truth. God sees the heart, and the heart should always be in right standing with God. So heed the red light, and **"stop."** Let peace rule your heart, and take time to check out the condition of your heart while waiting on the Lord. Secondly, the yellow light indicates to move slowly, with **"caution."** Be concerned enough to be watchful, examining everything to see if there is safety and security surrounding you before continuing. What is going on all around you? Develop the use of **"caution."** Seize time to look in the mirror, and check out who is looking back at you. You may be the one who needs to get "you" out of the way. Always look to where a thing will lead to, with consideration of the aftermath of the path you choose. Thirdly, the green light means **"go"** only if the signal of the Holy Spirit is leading you to proceed. Then, and only then, should you **"go,"** and only in the direction that you are being led to **"go."** If you are being led by your emotions, don't **"go."** Pray, and wait on the Lord to renew your strength. Then you will clearly see a difference. Think about the traffic light analogy to locate and examine yourself: red light, **"stop"**; yellow light, **"caution"**; and green light, **"go."** Recognize if you are having mere feelings, and be enlightened that God does not lead us by our feelings. He leads us by His Spirit.

For as many as are led by the Spirit of God, these are sons of God.

Romans 8:14

When life throws a bunch of sour grapes, lemons, or any heartbreaking or life-threatening experiences, know what Paul stated:

But we have this treasure in earthen vessels, that the excellence of the power may be of God and not of us. We are hard-pressed on every side, yet not crushed; we are perplexed, but not in despair; persecuted, but not forsaken; struck down, but not destroyed.

2 Corinthians 4:7-9

Whatever it may be that seems to want to leave a bitter taste in your life, get rid of it, and call on the name of the Lord, holding fast the confession of your faith without wavering.

What then shall we say to these things? If God is for us, who can be against us?

Romans 8:31

Yet in all these things we are more than conquerors through Him who loved us. For I am persuaded that neither death nor life, nor angels nor principalities nor powers, nor things present nor things to come, nor height nor depth, nor any other created thing, shall be able to separate us from the love of God which is in Christ Jesus our Lord.

Romans 8:37-39

We may get cast down, but we will not be conquered, for we are more than conquerors through Him who loved us. Don't allow the enemy to trick you into believing that no one loves or cares about you, for God is your

Refuge, your safe Place, and your Security, and it does not matter what may come at you. You have a Savior, and His name is Jesus. It's in Him that we live, and move, and have our being, and absolutely nothing can separate us from the love of God. Let's get it straight and put each in the proper place, and look at what Jesus said in the Scriptures:

> The thief does not come except to steal, and to kill, and to destroy. I have come that they may have life, and that they may have it more abundantly.
> John 10:10

In conclusion, I will "tell it"—how God is good all the time. He is merciful, loving, and kind, and His protection is upon our lives. Despite the consequences of life, God is always good, and it is never Him who causes anyone any harm, danger, trouble, sickness, or death. He is your Safe Place, Healer, Life Giver, Deliverer, Comforter, Protector, and Guide. He is gracious, merciful, kind, your Prince of Peace. He is everything you need. God is always good!

The test: Being trapped by the devil, his death row.

The trial: Sickness, persecutions, and death threats.

The testimony: I did not die, but lived to declare the works of the Lord.

Pray this prayer: *Father, You are my Refuge and my Fortress; You are my God, in whom I trust. I thank You for always being there for me. You are an on-time God, my Protector from hurt, harm, and danger. No weapon formed against me shall prosper, and the angel of the Lord encamps around me, for I reference You, Lord. Father, You have given me power over the works of the* *devil in the name of Jesus. When I feel weak, I am made strong in You. I am more than conquerors through Christ, who strengthens me. Cover me with Your feathers, and under Your wings I shall take refuge. I shall not be afraid of the terror by night, or of the arrow that flies by day, or of the pestilence that walks in darkness. Father, I ask You to keep me in all my ways, and in all my ways, I will acknowledge You. No evil shall befall me, and I will be aware of any tactics that may come up against me, my family, and anything concerning me. I overcome the world, the flesh, and the devil, for greater is He that is in me than he that is in the world. My help comes from You, Lord, who made the heavens and the earth. I praise Your holy name for Your mighty hand of protection over me. In Jesus' name I pray. Amen.*

The First and the Last

And He sat down, called the twelve, and said to them, "If anyone desires to be first, he shall be last of all and servant of all."

Mark 9:35

Jesus predicts His death and resurrection, letting the disciples know that the Son of man was about to be betrayed into the hands of men. He was not in denial of His deity as the Son of God; He was referring to his humanity as He spoke in Mark 9:31. Maybe the reason He made this reference was due to the fact that man can't destroy Him. He gave His life. He had taught the disciples while in Galilee that He would be killed and that after He was killed, He would rise on the third day. The disciples did not understand what Jesus was saying, and were afraid to ask Him. Sometime during their travel on the road from Galilee to Capernaum, the disciples were discussing who would be the greatest among them, with the anticipation of being "first" in the kingdom of heaven. Jesus asked them, "What was it that they disputed among themselves on the road, and why did they not answer Him?" Jesus, knowing all things, answered their dispute for them: "If anyone desires to be first, he shall be last of all and servant of all." Imagine that! To be first, you should be last, and servant of all. This scenario is true and apparent in today's world; people still love being "first." People everywhere in all walks of life have the desire to do extremely well, reflecting triumph in their lives. God, being a good God, wants you to excel in life; His desire is that you prosper.

> Let them shout for joy and be glad, who favor my righteous cause; and let them say continually, "Let the Lord be magnified, who has pleasure in the prosperity of His servant."
>
> Psalm 35:27

A desire for increase with the aim of being great is something that is good and of vital importance to mankind. Yet, it is almost impossible for anyone to successfully obtain greatness while at the same time smothering the good of serving others. A meaningful action of putting others first and serving them, while you consider yourself last, demonstrates unselfishness and the God kind of love. God's kingdom does not operate the same way the world's system operates. In the Lord's sight, if you desire to obtain first place, it is necessary that you become last. Parents will make sure their children are clothed and fed first, before parents clothe and feed themselves. They will make their children their first priority, possibly doing without themselves and putting their own needs last. When serving others first, you put yourself in position to be rewarded as being first because you made yourself last. The first will be last, and the last will be first; it's a role reversal in the kingdom of God. You are actually reaping the first place back unto yourself that you have sown in the course of giving it away. It puts you in a self-serving denial position with consideration of others, and shows unselfishness. You are not the center of your attention, but others are. I'm pretty sure many have found that they have put others' needs before their own. It is a servant's heart in service to others that keeps a person humble enough to do such a thing. Humility keeps pride out! Pride comes before a fall. If pride is there, there will be a fall. Many people who are in prominent high places, known to be first, find themselves reduced to a place of unimportance, being last. To keep their position, they must really be in service to others. If they are high-minded, they often fall. And many people who often end up being last in this lifetime are promoted to being of first and foremost importance, probably due to their humbleness, willingness to serve, and not looking to themselves. I used the word "many" because Jesus also clearly stated "many," not saying that *all* will:

> But many who are first will be last, and the last first.
>
> Matthew 19:30

Why did Jesus say "many"? I believe that in this instance, the word "many" is used to reflect that a man's heart is where his treasure is, just as Jesus counsels the rich young ruler, for he had great possessions and his heart was not willing to release his riches for the kingdom of heaven's cause. But later, when Jesus was talking with the disciples, He personalized it, using the word "he" to show that there was an individual choice. Not everyone will pay the price and choose to be last in service to others to be rewarded with the outcome, to become first. This clarifies that the word "many" means many, and not all, will choose to do so. God's way of doing things never ceases to amaze me. His ways are higher than our ways.

> "For My thoughts are not your thoughts, nor are your ways My ways," says the Lord. "For as the heavens are higher than the earth, so are My ways higher than your ways. And My thoughts than your thoughts"
>
> Isaiah 55:8-9

Sometimes in life, things are not always fair. People are not fair, and even God's ways that are not your ways can seem unfair, but His ways are mysteriously higher than our ways of doing things. It's best to trust Him and His ways of doing things. Remember, Father knows best. When giving up your way of doing things and trusting His way, you will see that it not only is beneficial to others, but will benefit you as well. You may experience having to sacrifice and give up some of your time to invest in others. Maybe with your job, you are doing most of the work, and it seems as if no one notices. Or you only have a few dollars with which to eat, and the Holy Spirit prompts you to give it away. Continue to do what is right and pleasing in God's sight, for God is a righteous God, and you will be rewarded. When we do things in our own ways, they are vain and will not produce the fruit that God can produce when things are done His way.

One day when we lived in our first home, the Lord led me to have a luncheon and to invite a few ladies from church. The day of the luncheon, the Lord told me I was not to eat, but to serve. I was hungry! I had planned, and had not eaten that morning, but because I love the Lord, I obeyed. The Lord had His plans for that day, on which His presence was truly manifested. There the glory came and saturated over us, the Holy Spirit used me to bring forth words from heaven. An act of obedience brought sensitivity to the Spirit of the Lord, all there could testify this truly was a word in due season. Lives were touched, and God was magnified. It was a beautiful, Spirit-filled luncheon having a great outcome on the day that the Lord had orchestrated. The next day in the Sunday morning church service, a confirmation of the same word spoken came forth by the Spirit of the Lord through the pastor. It's not about you, when you put God and others first.

People may be looked down upon because they are thought of as being last, normally not important or blessed. Let's look at what Jesus says will happen to them in the beatitudes:

- "Blessed are the poor in spirit, for theirs is the kingdom of heaven" (Matthew 5:3).
- "Blessed are those who mourn, for they shall be comforted" (Matthew 5:4).
- "Blessed are the meek, for they shall inherit the earth" (Matthew 5:5).
- "Blessed are those who hunger and thirst for righteousness, for they shall be filled" (Matthew 5:6).
- "Blessed are the merciful, for they shall obtain mercy" (Matthew 5:7).
- "Blessed are the pure in heart, for they shall see God" (Matthew 5:8).
- "Blessed are the peacemakers, for they shall be called sons of God" (Matthew 5:9).
- "Blessed are those who are persecuted for righteousness' sake, for theirs is the kingdom of heaven" (Matthew 5:10).
- "Blessed are you when they revile and persecute you, and say all kinds of evil against you falsely for My sake" (Matthew 5:11).
- "Rejoice and be exceedingly glad, for great is your reward in heaven, for so they persecuted the prophets who were before you" (Matthew 5:12).

The people in this description have humility and place themselves last in order to have quality in mannerism. They will have a reward in opposition to what they first had. People can be selfish without denying themselves the position of first place. If you want to be first, then be last and servant of all. I don't think Jesus is telling people not to love themselves, but not to love yourself any more than you can love another person.

Can you love your enemies, bless those who curse you, do what's good toward those who hate you, and pray for those who spitefully use you and persecute you? If your answer is yes, you are pleasing to God. When you look at the price Jesus paid, your price is only a light affliction. It really is not that hard at all to place yourself last when you are walking in the fruitfulness of love. Love looks at how it can be of service, getting its eye off of itself and seeing what it can do so someone else may enjoy and have a fulfilled life. You may be in the grocery store line, and things are going pretty slow with the cashier. Are you being pushy and complaining because you are in a hurry? Be patient, and consider that it may be that the cashier is new on the job, in training, and a bit nervous. When it is finally your turn to be served, try saying something pleasant that says you understand. Try encouraging the cashier not to worry. Things will turn around for the better. Get yourself off your mind, rid yourself of the "me first" mentality, and help others. There are many problems in our society because people are more concerned with themselves than they are with others. God does not want your good deeds done just so other people will see you and approve. He wants your goodwill service done from the heart, and it is He who will do the same for you.

> . . . not with eyeservice, as men-pleasers, but as bondservants of Christ, doing the will of God from the heart, with goodwill doing service, as to the Lord, and not to men, knowing that whatever good anyone does, he will receive the same from the Lord, whether he is a slave or free.
>
> Ephesians 6:6-8

> Therefore, whatever you want men to do to you, do also to them, for this is the Law and the Prophets.
>
> Matthew 7:12

We can change this world if we get rid of the "me first" mentality and put ourselves last. This is not to say that you are not to do anything for yourself, only that it should not be all about you. There are people who seldom or never attend church; you are to remember that it is the goodness of God that leads men unto repentance. Demonstrating the love of God through acts of kindness, prayer, laying hands on the sick, and consideration glorifies God and gives people the opportunity to come over to the Lord's side. You should always be looking for opportunities to serve God and others. When you are busy thinking about service in the kingdom of God, there's little time to be thinking too much about yourself. Long ago, neighbors knew one another; they borrowed cups of sugar, flour, and eggs. They would come over and help when there was a need or just to check to see how you were doing. There were many acts of compassion and kindness as a witness of God's goodness. Today, things have changed a lot in society. It appears that people barely know who their neighbors are or even know their names. Because of crime, workloads, busy schedules, and not trusting others, people have become somewhat secluded and have withdrawn inside their own shells of protection. This has limited the reaching out to make a difference in the lives of other people—even your neighbor who is living right next door to you. Thank God for the Holy Spirit, His Word, and His wisdom, which leads His children to continue to find ways to go about reconciling man to Christ Jesus and displaying His love.

Are you willing to obey God by placing yourself last so you become first? Let me recommend one way that you are able to put others first. That's in prayer. The Lord has led me to have prayer in my home for the last five years. There are a few other ladies who have joined in this prayer. With heartfelt prayer, we pray for all men, including you, the reader. Yes, we are praying for you because "all men" is all-inclusive, leaving no one out. Here is the foundation Scripture that we pray, and you can as well.

> Therefore I exhort first of all that supplications, prayers, intercessions, and giving of thanks be made for all men, for kings and all who are in authority, that we may lead a quiet and peaceable life in all godliness and reverence. For this is good and acceptable in the sight of God our Savior, who desires all men to be saved and to come to the knowledge of the truth. For there is one God and one Mediator between God and men, the Man Christ Jesus.
>
> 1 Timothy 2:1-5

Notice that in this epistle, the apostle Paul is encouraging supplications, prayers, and intercessions, and giving of thanks be made "first of all." The indication here is not "you" praying or mindful of yourself, but praying for others first, for all men, those in leadership and those who are in authority. Why is that? Men, kings, and those in authority are placed in leadership of others, or in the position of being first. When you pray for them to come into the knowledge of truth, the truth can be passed down to all who fall under their leadership and influence. And it is not God's will that any man should perish, but He desires "all men" to be saved and to come to the knowledge of the truth. I believe one of the best ways to help people is through the power of prayer. You cannot change man, but prayer activates the power of God to do the changing. Being in the position that God has allowed men to be in, there's a great responsibility that's required of them. Right before Paul encouraged us to pray "first of all" for all men, he told Timothy:

This charge I commit to you, son Timothy, according to the prophecies previously made concerning you, that by them you may wage the good warfare, having faith and a good conscience, which some having rejected, concerning the faith have suffered shipwreck, of whom are Hymenaeus and Alexander, whom I delivered to Satan that they may learn not to blaspheme.

1 Timothy 1:18-20

To blaspheme means to speak about God or sacred things with abuse or contempt, to rail at or revile with contumelious or insulting words or actions. It was after Paul stated this that he went on to encourage praying for "all men." He is exhorting us to pray for all men, with the anticipation of keeping anyone away from the spirit of blasphemy, in which Hymenaeus and Alexander had been involved. "Every sin and blasphemy will be forgiven men, but the blasphemy against the Spirit will not be forgiven men" (Matthew 12:31). It is good to practice not speaking ill of others, and to pray because "... the effective, fervent prayer of a righteous man avails much" (James 5:16). You can be more effective in the area of prayer. When it comes to people, God is able to do exceedingly above all that you can ask or think. He is able to turn the heart of a king.

The king's heart is in the hand of the Lord, like the rivers of water; He turns it wherever He wishes.

Proverbs 21:1

Pray instead of complaining about your husband, employer, pastor, government, king, queen, president, principal, teacher, police officers, and so on. True leaders are people of influence, not of power. Pray for them; pray for *all* men. No matter where you look, there are people who are leaders and people who follow, but

273

who really is the greatest? Jesus tells this truth of who is the greatest to the multitudes and to His disciples after telling them of the scribes and Pharisees wanting high positions. They were telling others what to do, yet they did not do, and they wanted their works to be seen by men. They were failing to be good examples of a leader pleasing in the sight of God. Jesus said:

But he who is greatest among you shall be your servant. And whoever exalts himself will be humbled, and he who humbles himself will be exalted.
                                              Matthew 23:11-12

When a person is in authority, it does not give him or her the right to dictatorship. The person has not been put in a position of leadership to have everyone at his or her beck and call, but to serve. A husband is one who is considered first, the head of the wife. He works hard at supplying the family needs before his own, and puts himself last. The husband's nature to put his family first and himself last is an illustrated attribute of the husband called the head (making himself last qualifies him to be first). When the "first becomes last," the "last becomes "first." Jesus, too, "did not come to be served, but to serve, and to give His life a ransom for many" (Matthew 20:28). Your works of service do not save you, but once saved, your life should become a life of service.

For by grace you have been saved through faith, and that not of yourselves; it is the gift of God, not of works, lest anyone should boast. For we are His workmanship, created in Christ Jesus for good works, which God prepared beforehand that we should walk in them.
                                              Ephesians 2:8-10

God has predestined for us to work in His service of serving others. The business world understands to be successful businesses, they must be of service to their customers. By serving others, you will develop a habit of thinking of the needs and considering the interests of others. It's easy to understand why in God's sight the people who put themselves last are first, because it demonstrates an extraordinary love in the direction of someone else, not selfishness. I believe that when you demonstrate the principle of first becoming last, you represent what He is—the First and the Last, the Alpha and the Omega. Every believer has the opportunity to serve, but it's a matter of choice. Are you willing to go the extra mile and be of service to others? Sometimes take the focus off of your busy life, and help someone else along in life. You will feel more centered and fulfilled.

Jesus' biblical expression in Matthew 23:11 expresses that he who *is* the greatest shall be your servant. With a willing and humble heart, anyone is capable of attaining the right in God's sight to be first by becoming last. God's ways of doing things are higher and much different from the ways one may hope for things to be done. If you desire to be first, you must learn to serve, placing yourself last with a willing and humble heart. To be first in the sight of God is to be last, just as being last in God's sight is being first. You may not get the recognition from man that you feel you should, but know that God sees all. You should not be in service for man to behold anyway. Your service is unto the Lord God. Stay faithful, knowing that your work, your labor of love, is not in vain.

The test: Putting yourself last and being of service to others first.

The trial: Denying and forgetting about yourself while giving first place to another.

The testimony: The first and greatest in the sight of God by becoming last and serving others first in this world.

Pray this prayer: *Father, I thank You that I am in service to others. I ask You to keep me meek, with a heart that continually hungers and thirsts after righteousness. You are my First and Last. You are the Alpha and Omega, the Beginning and the End. Create within me a pure heart, that I may serve in Your work here on the earth, whereby You are pleased, and that I look not to man to reward me, but I look to You, my heavenly Father, to reward me. I seek to please You, and for You to receive all the glory done in my life. Thank You for Jesus' teachings in this area of the First and the Last. You are my everything, and it is You that I serve. In Jesus' name I pray. Amen.*

Knowing

O Lord, You have searched me and known me.
You know my sitting down and my rising up; You
understand my thought afar off.

Psalm 139:1-2

You have hedged me behind and before, and laid
Your hand upon me. Such knowledge is too wonderful for me; it is high, I cannot attain it.

Psalm 139:5-6

God is omniscient, or *all-knowing*. He knows everything, and man cannot hide from Him or ever
obtain all that He is. The best way to know God is to
spend time with Him, and when you do so, He will reveal
Himself unto you. How much of Him do you want to see
and know? Moses spent time with God, and he was only
allowed to look and see His back, to behold just *some* of
who God is. Man in the flesh cannot handle such mag-
nificence. God's radiance is so glorious that if you only
had a peek at Him, you would become saturated with
such splendor that your sinful nature couldn't handle
it. The flesh would collapse and die if it stood in such
wonder; the flesh can't handle such power. Moses was
an example of that. God allowed only His goodness, His
glory to pass before Moses, for the Bible says no man
can see His face and live.

Then He said, "I will make all My goodness pass before you, and I will proclaim the name of the Lord before you. I will be gracious to whom I will be gracious, and I will have compassion on whom I will have compassion." But He said, "You cannot see My face; for no man shall see Me, and live."

Exodus 33:19-20

So it shall be, while My glory passes by, that I will put you in the cleft of the rock, and will cover you with My hand while I pass by. Then I will take away My hand, and you shall see My back; but My face shall not be seen.

Exodus 33:22-23

Imagine God being *so* good and glorious that seeing no more than His back gave an adequate amount of goodness, a sufficient amount of His glory. My, my, my! I have to stop for a moment and glorify the Lord. HALLELUJAH, Lord, I praise You for all that You are, all of Your goodness, all of Your glory! My soul magnifies You! There is no other like You! You are God! You are magnificent in all Your splendor and glory! You are wonderful! I adore You! You are the King of kings and Lord of lords! You are the Alpha and Omega, the Beginning and the End! You are God, and there is no other! You are Lord, and I love You. Glory to God in the highest, for He is good.

Knowing God's Word

Long ago when I worked and had rededicated my life to the Lord, I wanted to know Him personally. I began to read my Bible from the beginning to the end, captivated by the Word and the power of it. I was awestruck. My husband and I had not yet started a family; it was just the two of us. Every time I had an opportunity, I would read the Bible. I literally spent all of my spare time reading the Bible. Morning, afternoon, and night, if I had no work to do or was not at church, I was reading the Bible. During my work breaks, I seldom went to the breakroom, so I might salvage every minute of my time and read the Bible. Time was valuable. During my fifteen-minute break or forty-five-minute lunchtime, I would grab my Bible and sit at my work station and read. It was my season of learning and knowing Him. I hungered so for the Word and remember saying, "Lord, I'm greedy, and I want all of You." I heard just as real in my spirit, "You can't handle all of Me." I thought, *Why?*

He showed me one day by allowing me to experience something while taking my break. That particular day, I did go to the breakroom, and as I was reading the Bible, I was saturated with His presence. His anointing covered me. I knew His Spirit was upon me, but I did not understand at the time all that was going on. What I knew was I felt wonderful; I felt like rays of light constantly flowed from my body. It was so wonderful and powerful. It felt good, radiant, and bright like the sun when it bursts forth its glimmer. It was so splendid that I closed my Bible and literally felt as if my spirit were about to exit my body. It was a glorious feeling. It was so glorious that I shook myself and resisted it because I knew something was about to take place, and I didn't know what. Imagine having that much goodness overtake you to the point that you are so overwhelmed that you feel you have to leave your body. That's exactly how it felt. There was no fear at all. Due to not knowing what was happening, I resisted it. Then I heard, "You just quenched the Spirit." And I knew I should not be resisting this strongly felt Spirit of God, but I was not sure what was taking place at that time. The Spirit of God was working; maybe He was going to allow me to have an out-of-body experience and go into a trance like Peter did:

Then he became very hungry and wanted to eat; but while they made ready, he fell into a trance and saw heaven opened and an object like a great sheet bound at the four corners, descending to him and let down to the earth.

Acts 10:10-11

Was God about to show me something, as He did Peter? I don't know because I resisted. God, through His Spirit, taught me whenever we resist the presence of His Spirit, His power is reduced from manifestation. The glory of the Lord is real, and others can see and know when you have been in the presence of the Lord. One day when I was walking down the aisle at work, a guy hurried toward me and said, "You are just glowing." I responded, "It's the Lord." I knew this guy really saw something. I felt it! I felt a beam of light coming from my body like the rays that come from the sun. The Lord told me this is what they saw on Moses when he came down from Mount Sinai with the two tablets. After Moses had been in the presence of God, the skin of his face shone; he actually put a veil on his face to cover it. I had been in the Word every spare minute that I had, whether at work or at home curled up on the sofa for long hours. It was the Word, the Word, and the Word for me. The Word and God are one and the same; therefore, being constantly in the Word of God, I was submerged in God's presence, and His glory shone from my face. Being constantly in the Word of God is being in His presence. As I stated earlier, I didn't understand it all at the time, but I sure enjoyed it. It was also like being in heaven. There was a knowing that God was with me in power, to taste and see that the Lord is good.

Years later, I felt that same strong sense of being saturated by God, and then I said, "Lord, what do I do with this?" I heard, "You can't handle it all. You have to release the anointing power on others." Another day,

His presence again came strong while I was in church. I shook someone's hand, and what literally felt like electricity came from my hand. I knew that was the power of God, and I asked the person, "Did you feel that?" That person did not, but I know power left me and imparted into that person. It is not all the time that I sense His power upon me with such saturation, but I know when He is present, and having come into more knowledge of His ways and with the leading of the Holy Spirit, I believe the time will come when God will pay me another visit to demonstrate His power, that His will be done.

When you are in the Word of God, you are in Him; you will come to know Him and all His glory. Knowing God's Word is knowing Him. You cannot separate one from the other, for He and His Word are one and the same.

> In the beginning was the Word, and the Word was with God, and the Word was God.
>
> John 1:1

It is important to spend time in the Word of God; you will find Him there. Knowing God's Word will keep you in any given situation. If you have the Word, you have God! Want a survival kit? Take these two for endurance: the Word of God and the Holy Spirit. Jesus knew the importance of God's Word, to keep Him. He was the Word in the flesh. He could not be tricked by the devil, who spoke the Word out of context to Jesus. Don't accept any trickery from the devil. Know the Word for yourself! It's the knowing that will keep you from being deceived. Let's look a bit more into the tempter coming to tempt Jesus, as if He didn't know any better.

> Then Jesus was led up by the Spirit into the wilderness to be tempted by the devil. And when He had fasted forty days and forty nights, afterward

He was hungry. Now when the tempter came to Him, he said, "If You are the Son of God, command that these stones become bread." But He answered and said, "It is written, 'Man shall not live by bread alone, but by every word that proceeds from the mouth of God.'"

Matthew 4:1-4

When you have the Word of God residing on the inside of you, and the tempter comes to test you, as he did Jesus, draw out and speak the Word of God, for it is powerful. Having the Word of God in you and speaking it does not mean the devil will immediately stop his temptation. Not only will he not stop immediately, he may attempt to use the Word of God continually on you, as he did with Jesus.

Then the devil took Him up into the holy city; set Him on the pinnacle of the temple, and said to Him, "If You are the Son of God, throw Yourself down. For it is written: 'He shall give His angels charge over you,' and, 'In their hands they shall bear you up, lest you dash your foot against a stone.'"

Matthew 4:5-6

If the devil is ever speaking to you, know that he is still up to his same old tricks of deception. Know that Jesus came that you might have life, and whenever the devil speaks, don't believe him, as he comes to steal, kill, and destroy. There is deception and trickery behind whatever he speaks, for he is a liar, the father of lies. The devil is a deceiver, so believe nothing that comes from him. The devil will try to keep you from the Word of God with cares of the world and other distractions. He also wants to get you separated from fellowship with other believers so he can attempt to poison you with his lies and deceptions. He took Jesus into the holy city and seated him on a pinnacle, a little wing, at a high peak that rises above the roof of a building. This wing has been regarded as the apex, meaning the highest point of the sanctuary. The devil wanted Jesus to cast Himself down from this pinnacle. His trick was for Jesus to kill Himself, to commit suicide, so to speak, so that Jesus would not fulfill His purpose. But he could not trick Jesus because Jesus knows all things; He was the living Word (John 1:10-18). He was then and is today the greater One, and He cannot be tempted. No one can entice Him to do wrong.

Are you going to allow the tempter to have you do something like jump and take your own life, so it would be said that you committed suicide? Imagine yourself high up on a pinnacle, possibly as high as three mountain-tops, with a thought coming to your mind to jump. After the thought, you hear the words, "He shall give His angels charge concerning you and in their hands they shall bear you up, lest at any time you dash your foot against a stone." You may feel as if no one cares, and you may even want to take your life—put a gun to your head or overdose on pills. But don't do it! Jesus came that you might have life, not death. Thoughts of taking your life, or any thoughts contrary to a good, full, and satisfied life, are not from the Lord. If you should have any negative thoughts of defeat or destruction, cast those thoughts down. Call a friend or someone else to minister life-encouraging words to you, to help pull you in the right direction. You are not to obey words that are not God's will.

> Let no one say when he is tempted, "I am tempted by God"; for God cannot be tempted by evil, nor does He Himself tempt anyone.
>
> James 1:13

God will in no way tempt anyone with evil. It's always the devil that tempts people with evil, and anything that is evil or a wrongdoing is never from God. If an evil thought is constant, be like Jesus, and speak more of God's Word and rebuke the devil, as Jesus did, when needed. The devil continued with his tactic until Jesus rebuked him:

> Then Jesus said to him, "Away with you, Satan! For it is written, 'You shall worship the Lord your God, and Him only you shall serve.'"
>
> Matthew 4:10

It was after Jesus rebuked him that the devil left Him. You, too, have been given authority over all the works of the devil, in the name of Jesus, and you do not have to be deceived by him. The devil must have thought Jesus was physically weak enough to give in to his tricks because Jesus had fasted for forty days and was hungry. Like Jesus, don't give in to the devil's offers during times when you feel weak, unloved, or unimportant, or are despairing. It is a trap to ensnare you, and will be brought to light, mocking you. And don't think that what you do wrong in secret will stay hidden:

> For there is nothing hidden which will not be revealed, nor has anything been kept secret, but that it should come to light. If anyone has ears to hear, let him hear.
>
> Mark 4:22-23

Don't be deceived and tricked into thinking you are getting away with anything that is a wrongdoing. Because no one sees you, it may appear you are being concealed in secret. However, that's the devil's way of doing his job to lead you to destruction. He will make you think you are getting away with what's being done in secret. But rest assured, one day it will manifest in the light. We see this happen a lot in the world around us. There are many things that were hidden that have manifested in the light for all to see. Be sober, be diligent, and do not allow the devil to devour you. Knowing and obeying God's Word will make a difference in your life. Know that no matter what the test, the Word of God is powerful and effectual, when you heed and obey the Word, you will pass the test. Knowing and applying the Word of God will help you in your everyday walk because you will be aware of anything that is in opposition to it.

Knowing God's Voice

God has given us the Holy Spirit, who ultimately leads and guides us today. God communicates with us by His Holy Spirit, just as Peter heard Him when he was in the city of Joppa praying. Peter explained his reasons to those who had contended with him for going to uncircumcised men and eating with them. Peter let them know what had happened to him when he went into a trance and saw in a vision "an object descending like a great sheet, let down from heaven by four corners; and it came to" him. He saw "four-footed animals of the earth, wild beasts, creeping things, and birds of the air" and heard a voice speaking to him (Acts 11:4-6).

> And I heard a voice saying to me, "Rise, Peter; kill and eat." But I said, "Not so, Lord! For nothing common or unclean has at any time entered my mouth." But the voice answered me again from heaven, "What God has cleansed you must not call common." Now this was done three times, and all were drawn up again into heaven.
>
> Acts 11:7-10

Man seldom or never hears the audible voice of God Himself, but invariably will hear what God is saying through the Holy Spirit. Whenever the Holy Spirit speaks, He will not speak of Himself, but only what He hears coming from the Father through the Son. Jesus said:

> However, when He, the Spirit of truth, has come, He will guide you into all truth; for He will not speak on His own authority, but whatever He hears He will speak; and He will tell you things to come. He will glorify Me, for He will take of what is Mine and declare it to you.
>
> John 16:13-14

Everything that comes from the Holy Spirit is coming from the Father, who sent the Son. There is an order here. The Father, the Son, and the Holy Spirit are working together in unison. In the beginning, God did His works by and through Himself. He later sent His Son, Jesus, who, in His appointed time on earth, finished what He was commissioned to do. And now He has sent His Holy Spirit, who, through Him, for all intents and purposes, is universal. He can be in believers all over the world at the same time. Jesus came in the flesh and was limited physically in where he could be at one time. In His whereabouts, the Holy Spirit is not limited; therefore, God has Him, the Holy Spirit, as His spokesperson to believers. Believers who are widespread are being led everywhere, listening to the voice of the Lord by His Spirit and giving God the glory. Do you know when it is God who is truly speaking to you, or if it's a stranger's voice? Whenever you hear the voice of your spouse or child, with whom you live daily, you are familiar with it. You are able to distinguish their voices from any other voices that you may hear in a room. Why is that? You know them; you reside with them, day in and day out; you hear their voices on a regular basis. If someone should call out to you to come to him or her with the pretense that the person is your spouse or child, you will not follow the voice because it's the voice of a stranger. The shepherd knows his sheep, and they know his voice.

> To him the doorkeeper opens, and the sheep hear his voice; and he calls his own sheep by name and leads them out. . . . I am the good shepherd; and I know My sheep, and am known by My own. . . . And other sheep I have which are not of this fold; them also I must bring, and they will hear My voice; and there will be one flock and one shepherd.
>
> John 10:3, 14, 16

> My sheep hear My voice, and I know them, and they follow Me.
>
> John 10:27

The shepherd and the sheep know one another. Whose voice are you following? Jesus said His sheep "hear" His voice; He knows them, and they follow Him. An intimate relationship has to be developed. One must have been born again into the family of God. Just as a child becomes acquainted with his or her parent's voice, smell, and ways of doing things, so do the shepherd's sheep become acquainted with His voice, His sweet fragrance, and His ways of doing things. Listen, and know when the Spirit of the Lord is speaking to you, and follow no other. His voice will not lead you in a way that opposes the written Word of God. He is not going to tell you to lie, steal, or kill, or that someone else's spouse is your spouse, which is coveting. He is not going to tell you to deceive, cheat, practice sorcery, or hate your brother or sister, nor will He put sickness on you. This does not glorify God. Those things listed are all works from the enemy. How can any of these glorify God when He is good? Your natural parents don't put sickness on you, nor do they desire for you to partake in any of the above wrong things. God is not in evil or any wrongdoings. He does not cohere in agreement with any of it. In knowing God's voice, you will know the difference. Instead of doing all the talking in prayer, take time and listen. You can't hear the Holy Spirit speak if you are always doing the talking. Two keys to knowing His voice is to know His Word and His Spirit. Remember, with Elijah, it was a "still small voice" (1 Kings 19:11-13).

Do You Not Know?

Whenever Paul asks, "Do you not know?" he is implying that you should know. Let's look at several verses where he asks the same question, "Do you not know?" He first started asking this question because they were not to sue the brethren, taking them to court to settle things when they themselves should know how to judge and handle things among themselves.

Dare any of you, having a matter against another, go to law before the unrighteous, and not before the saints? . . . Do you not know that we shall judge angels? How much more, things that pertain to this life?

1 Corinthians 6:1, 3

Paul is saying, How are we to judge angels when we will not judge matters among one another and things that concern us in this life? As Christians, we should have love and the knowledge of how to make amends to bring us back in the love walk and peace with one another. He asks this question again, saying we should know things that are wrongdoings:

288

Do you not know that the wicked will not inherit the kingdom of God? Do not be deceived: Neither the sexually immoral nor idolaters nor adulterers nor male prostitutes nor homosexual offenders nor thieves nor the greedy nor drunkards nor slanderers nor swindlers will inherit the kingdom of God.

1 Corinthians 6:9-10 NIV

Do you not know that your bodies are members of Christ? Shall I then take the members of Christ and make them members of a harlot? Certainly not! Or do you not know that he who is joined to a harlot is one body with her? For "the two," He says, "shall become one flesh." But he who is joined to the Lord is one spirit with Him. Flee sexual immorality. Every sin that a man does is outside the body, but he who commits sexual immorality sins against his own body.

1 Corinthians 6:15-18

Or do you not know that your body is the temple of the Holy Spirit who is in you, whom you have from God, and you are not your own? For you were bought at a price; therefore glorify God in your body and in your spirit, which are God's.

1 Corinthians 6:19-20

These were things that Paul felt the body of Christ should know. If you did not know these things and you are reading them now, you have come into knowledge of the truth of the Word of God. Like it or not, it is the written Word, and it is what it is, and you are to glorify God in body and also in spirit.

Christians should ever be learning the Word of God and His way of doing things. When you come into the kingdom of God, you are to be growing in the knowledge

289

of truth. Make sure you find a local church assembly that teaches the Word of God and demonstrates His Spirit. If you have challenges in your flesh and are not able to control the flesh, nourish yourself with the Word of God. It is how you will grow. You are to desire it, like a child desires to be fed milk. If you are not hungry enough to be fed spiritually, you will become stagnant and inactive in the body of Christ and not grow.

> Therefore, laying aside all malice, all deceit, hypocrisy, envy, and all evil speaking, as new-born babes, desire the pure milk of the word, that you may grow thereby.
>
> 1 Peter 2:1-2

All fleshly deeds are to be laid aside, and you are to desire the pure milk of the Word. If you want to grow spiritually, you need to be fed the Word of God. Throughout the Bible, you can find Scriptures that knowing is relevant. As a matter of fact, God says His people are destroyed for the lack of knowledge. Why? They rejected it without wanting to increase in knowledge.

> My people are destroyed for lack of knowledge. Because you have rejected knowledge, I also will reject you from being priest for Me; because you have forgotten the law of your God, I also will forget your children.
>
> Hosea 4:6

God was speaking to the children of Israel, for they had no mercy or knowledge of Him in the land. They were swearing, lying, killing, stealing, and also committing adultery. They were more inclined to doing flesh acts than coming into the knowledge of truth so that they could be kept. Their priorities were not right, and they were being destroyed by their own deeds. They were following their way of doing things and not increasing in the knowledge of the truth of God's ways of doing things.

In today's society, people are always learning and never coming into the knowledge of the truth of God's Word. They are constantly rejecting truth and feeding their own fleshly desires. Thank God that as Christians, we have the opportunity to pray for all men, every one of them, excluding none, to come into the knowledge of truth. As mentioned in the last chapter, Paul urges us to do so:

> Therefore I exhort first of all that supplications, prayers, intercessions, and giving of thanks be made for all men, for kings and all who are in authority, that we may lead a quiet and peaceable life in all godliness and reverence. For this is good and acceptable in the sight of God our Savior, who desires all men to be saved and to come to the knowledge of the truth.
>
> 1 Timothy 2:1-4

I discussed this in the last chapter, "The First and the Last," and explained that one way to put others first was by praying for them. I'm now using this same text from the stance of, **"Do you not know?"** **"Do you not know"** that God wants you to pray for all men, no matter their lot in life? As Christians, you are to pray for them. **"Do you not know"** the more you pray for all men, the more compassion you will have toward them and the less you'll be concerned with what they may be doing? You cannot pray with the belief that you have what you've asked, and then speak in contradiction of that or even speak ill of anyone. **"Do you not know"** that praying will steer you clear from murmuring and complaining? **"Do you not know"** you will become affected as you are praying for others, that there's a boomerang effect causing you to change? You will see people in the way that God sees them, and have the same love, mercy, kindness, and compassion. **"Do you not know"** that without the Lord, people are lost? They are in need of enlightenment. **"Do you not know"** we are not to love sins and wrongdoings, but we are to love sinners? God does. It is not His will that any man should perish, but that all should come to the knowledge of the truth. **"Do you not know"** while we are here on this earth, we are to do all that we can to win this world for Christ? Are you willing to count all things lost for the excellence of the knowledge of Christ Jesus? Knowing the truth will liberate you and increase you for so much more. Study and be a doer of the Word of God, stay in the knowledge of the truth, be set free and your life will change. And remember to pray.

The test: Getting to know the Lord God and His way of doing things.

The trial: Facing distractions that can take you away from the presence of the Lord.

The testimony: Having come into the knowledge of the truth, whereby you are able to stand on God's Word and see it come alive in your life!

Pray this prayer: *Father, I thank You for making Your Word available for me, that I may grow by it. I ask You to cause me through the study of Your Word to continue into Your knowledge of truth, to apply in my life Your way of doing things. I am Your child, I know Your voice, and I will not follow a strange voice leading me to anything that is contrary to Your Word. I will position myself to read Your Word, and to hunger and thirst after righteousness, that I may be filled. I will desire the sincere milk of the Word, that I may grow by it. Thank You for* *allowing me to come into the knowledge of praying for all men, that they, too, may come into the knowledge of Your truth and be set free. I ask You that people not reject the knowledge of Your truth when it comes his or her way. Keep me ever walking in the path of righteousness. Thank You, Father. I believe I have what I have asked. In Jesus' name I pray. Amen.*

9 781612 157528